NEW YORK:
Confidential!

NEW YORK: Confidential!

by

JACK LAIT
and
LEE MORTIMER

New Revised Edition

CROWN PUBLISHERS, Inc. · NEW YORK

PRINTED IN THE UNITED STATES OF AMERICA
AMERICAN BOOK–KNICKERBOCKER PRESS, INC., NEW YORK

CONTENTS

CONTENTS

vi

INTRODUCTION

P-*S-S-T*—

Lait and Mortimer want a word with you—confidential:

The authors had a lot of fun writing these pages. And infinitely more getting what they put into them. They both turned prematurely gray becoming Broadway-wise.

What you will read here they observed, absorbed, inhaled and swallowed through the years. They lived it.

This tome has no message. It may be helpful, it may be useful, but never purposeful, though it attempts to offer much sound advice. But who ever followed sound advice? If folks did, there would be no more marriages, divorces, gambling, guzzling, dancing, romancing, chasing, cheating, slickers, suckers, hussies, hangmen or hangovers—heaven forbid!

The "Confidential" in the title means Lait and Mortimer, who have never been in Grant's Tomb, have been in a lot of other places not so roomy, gloomy or wide open. It means they got their stuff off the record and on the up-and-up.

Therefore, this is not for Aunt Katie from Keokuk, but Uncle Dave the Deacon might find it of value next time he attends a convention in New York.

If you are seeking an orthodox guide or travel book about Gotham, lay this down. You will find little about the Empire State Building, Brooklyn Bridge or the $2.50 cruise around Manhattan. The shelves of stores and libraries already groan under the burden of books on those subjects.

No. This is a commentary on and compendium of the Big Burg from the inside out, with some facts and observations that could amaze, amuse and steer not only strangers, but most of those supposedly nonexistent Americans, native New Yorkers.

The gaucherie of many locals as well as all yokels defies the emery-wheel polish of the world's most exciting, most thrilling and most misunderstood metropolis.

The cognoscenti—you can count them on the keys of the piano that Polly Adler stored when, after 40 years of lucrative operation of the oldest profession, she quit and went to Hollywood—know a few things, but their experiences have been circumscribed. Knowing New York is a full-time career.

To those who still get dizzy looking up at the tall buildings, who think a headwaiter smiles at them because he likes them, who send notes back to the stage-door tender and who think this is just Milwaukee multiplied, we cheerfully dedicate the memory of our mornings after and aspirins thereafter. We will them the thousands of waking hours when we should have been asleep, as lagniappe.

But we believe that if our readers study this work assiduously and note its findings and one-way arrows, they may avoid some booby-traps. We believe so, though we don't expect so.

If this volume has any aim, it has four. It is designed to tip off the frequent visitor, who "knows" his New

York; to derube the first-timer or the once-in-a-whiler; to polish up the permanent resident, who is sure he knows "our town"; and to give the largest classification, the vicarious traveler who does his New York sightseeing at home, in his easy chair, a series of close-ups that he never ogled off a screen or Sunday supplement.

We shoot at all ages, sexes and checkbooks. To them we present an island, hard, hostile, palms up and thumbs down—but hot.

Its creed is cash. Don't try to crash it otherwise.

You can't buy everything—only almost everything.

And it's worth all it costs you if you buy the right merchandise in the right spot at the right time.

That's why we were born, to tell you about it—confidential.

PART ONE

THE PLACES
(*Confidential!*)

1. MY LITTLE GAY HOME IN THE EAST

THIS LITTLE island called Manhattan is the summer resort supreme.

Never a mosquito, rarely a fly is seen.

Millions live high, where it's cool and rather quiet, except for the soothing and varied whistles of the boats and an occasional fire or police siren.

You don't have to be sociable with heterogeneous strangers or even your party-wall neighbors, whom you seldom know on sight.

If you want to sail, there are two magnificent rivers, the broad and sporting Sound and the most breath-stopping harbor on earth.

If you want mountains, you go by magic elevators to the observatories in the Chrysler Building, Radio City or the Empire State, where you get a magnificent view as soon as the suicides clear the railings.

There are, even in mid-July, two score legitimate theatres offering the great hits, for shows that survive into this period are all lusty and hardy. Within easy drives are locality playhouses with several other sturdy attractions, and "straw hat" tryout and revival productions. You have a wide choice of concerts, indoor and outdoor opera, a dozen swanky or swift cabarets and a hundred minor ones.

There are three big-league baseball teams within a $1.50 taxi hop from Times Square, always one and

3

often two at home, all exciting, usually at least one out in front.

There are a half-dozen boxing shows each week, al-fresco or, like most of the burg, air-conditioned.

If you would attend churches, we have some of the finest and most famous cathedrals of all faiths and creeds.

Half the saloons are equipped with television, and for the price of a beer you can see and hear leading sports and other biff-bang affairs as they are proceeding.

There are eating places from sub-sub basements to the 85th floor, and from automats where you slip in a coin and get back a hot hamburger to the Stork and El Morocco, where you won't be allowed in, which is just as well for your bank roll.

There are sidewalk cafés, acres of penthouse-terrace restaurants, menus and service and customs of all na-tions, including the Scandinavian and not excluding the Moravian.

And, summer or any season, you have a feeling that the world is spinning about you—and whole little worlds, not geared just for tourists—concentrations of all nations and segments of them—even a White Russian colony.

Taxis galore drop the flag at 20 cents. The average haul is a half-buck.

Everything is big time. There's an air and a snap and a tang to Manhattan that is generated by cham-pionship rather than by huge mobilizations of people and of money. Brooklyn is far more populous; Chicago has more than twice the population. But there is a zip and a zing here, a supercivilized, metropolitan method of behavior, unique and indescribable.

Manhattan has a nonchalance about the world and itself known nowhere else. The newspapers do not bother to publish the borough's own vital statistics. One can be born, married, have children, die and be buried, entirely unnoticed. At the other extreme, nobody is important. Celebrities get a passing glance, maybe, and not always that.

Bank statements list billions in deposits and almost no one reads them. Ships from every port come and go and get a line for the record, in a few gazettes.

Yet there is civic pride, there are organized boosters; Rotarians and Kiwanians and Lions meet and slap backs and call one another Pete and Baldy.

No visitor can catch "the Voice of the City." O. Henry, who called it that, didn't. Nor can readers of the beloved tales of Damon Runyon. Damon was our friend and we admired him profoundly, because he could write fascinatingly, almost entirely from imagination, not from photographic impression. Characters like those he concocted never lived, around "Mindy's" or anywhere else. He laughingly said so, himself.

New Yorkers compose plays about New York and any resemblance to the living or dead is carelessness.

In truth, Manhattan—which for most fact or fiction material is New York—cannot be transcribed or translated.

It isn't even itself!

There are so many foreign and unrelated elements undergoing a steady, invisible process of blending; the picture changes slowly, yet ceaselessly; and no human camera is fast enough to catch it in the static focus of repose.

No one has portrayed New York as Dickens did London or Sue did Paris.

Those who tried have had to sectionalize it; none could wrap it all up into a comprehensive entity.

If they grasped the financial or theatrical or criminal or social or artistic or political aspect of the city's life, they could not extend the panorama into the human, the domestic, the personal phases.

If they looked on high they were so spellbound they could not turn to grope into the subterranean.

Those who realized the astounding things and people could not vitalize the humble, the ordinary, the devout and industrious bread-and-butter brothers and sisters.

Manhattan doesn't materialize to even those who spend their lives in it.

A thrilling, throbbing mystery!

2. THE CANYON

DAMON RUNYON immortalized 47th Street, between Sixth and Seventh Avenues, as "Dream Street." Jack Lait dramatized it as "The Canyon."

It is a shabby, dismal block. Its 200 yards are lined almost unbrokenly by cheap hotels and rooming houses sheltering all manner of strange characters: retired vaudevillians, down-and-out horse-players, dope fiends, grifters and grafters, pickpockets, derelicts (male and female), drunks, stage widows, miserly recluses, tars and their tarts, crap-game steerers and bottom-dealers.

On fine days you see them on the sidewalks. Old women with grotesque young get-ups and peroxided hair, parading their pooches; bewhiskered, unkempt men on the church steps, passionately studying racing scratch sheets; apoplectic dipsomaniacs airing out cheap jags; actors whose world has gone by, talking of starring roles of the past—and next season.

Here is the stage door of the once fabulous Palace, mecca for all vaudevillians. The theatre, pride of its builder, Martin Beck, was the hub of the old Keith-Orpheum Circuit, and on its stage appeared, for a quarter of a century, the top names of show business.

Around the corner is Broadway and the Great White Way.

A block to the east is prosperous Fifth Avenue, glistening in mink and pearls.

7

But life on Dream Street goes on, oblivious of these other worlds.

You may walk it at any hour. No one will molest you.

Maybe a panhandler will try to mooch a quarter; maybe a flea-bitten, superannuated sister in sin will make a half-hearted signal to you that she can be had. But you won't be in danger.

What goes on upstairs, in those small, old rooms, is something else. There crime and vice and con games and watering whiskey and hypoing horses are hatched.

There adultery is accepted as a fact of life.

There people who work are regarded as outlandish and queer.

But there you find no sluggers, stickups or bullies.

These are kindly folk. Violence is not in their bag of tricks.

This is, rather, a community. The members recognize the right to steal, to cheat, to beg, to scheme, to mate, and to woo weird fancies with hooch and hop.

But, no disorder, please—this is The Canyon!

* * *

Yet in the midst of this murk and muck, grew a flower.

Not a peony, not even a rose; a violet, gentle and shrinking and modest, admired and worshiped, but doomed to be crushed by the heavy hobnailed boots of the ruthless underworld and the equally pitiless protagonists of respectability.

In the middle of that bleak block, in a second-story apartment, lived big, hearty Martha Geiss. She was a one-bottle and one-case bootleggers' stock exchange. She didn't handle the stuff herself, but she had worked up a trade in hotels and offices, so small buyers 'phoned her when they wanted something sent up quickly, day or night, and she in turn relayed the orders to the various petty peddlers of gin and what was supposed to be whiskey.

Her commissions were never large and her work was wearisome and confining. But she always laughed and always had enough to help others and to act as a sort of mother to all the neighbors. And she was a mother— the mother of Frances, the only thing clean and virtuous and young and lovely on Dream Street.

When 200-pound Martha parted with her husband and cast her lot with the lawbreakers she brought with her the child, who went to a school in the slums west of Broadway.

Everybody knew her and everybody protected her. Youngsters were a great novelty in those parts and Frances was an unusually winsome and friendly one.

No one around there would harm her or let anyone else even say a questionable word that she might hear.

She was physically precocious and at 14 was a ripe, full-blown beauty, shy, courteous, simply but tastily dressed. Martha's heart was set on having Frances become a schoolteacher.

Of course, the child had eyes and ears—very pretty ones. She knew that this was no kindergarten in which she lived. She saw the liquor and dope-pushers, the demi-mondes and the semi-men. She smiled at them all and they smiled back, but as close as they were to her they were far away.

In the summer vacation, when Frances was 16, going to high school, Martha's business was rather low. It always fell off in summer, when many of the customers were in the country. Frances was eager to do her share, but Martha hated to send her into the world, where, strangely, she would not get the sheltering care and affection which had always been hers on dirty, degraded Dream Street. Across the way from Martha's window, where she could look into it on summer nights, was an Italian restaurant. Caruso, the owner, was her friend and at times her customer. She suggested that he hire Frances during the vacation as a checkroom and cigarette girl.

The patronage was not of the richest, but she did fairly well, what with her beauty and affability. Then, one night, she was called to a private dining room upstairs, where some men were secluded in what seemed to be a heavy conference. At the head of the table sat a stocky, blond, not bad-looking fellow in his thirties, who bought a fistful of cigars and reached for a $10 bill. As he looked up he saw the girl—then he reached for a $20 bill.

Later he came down and went on the make. She turned away and told him she never went out with men. He laughed and asked her:

"Do you know who I am?"

She shook her light brown curls from side to side.

He put his face very close to her ear and said huskily: "I am Dutch Schultz!"

10

In every walk of human life there is an upper class. Among the lifers in Alcatraz, who never again will freely see the light of God's sun or draw a free breath, there are classes. A man who has killed three cops looks down upon a piker who only kidnaped a child or robbed a post office.

The name he whispered had an electric effect. Among the prohibition aristocracy none stood as high as Arthur Flegenheimer, a tough boy from Yonkers, who not only controlled a large section of the beer business of New York but was the king of the policy racket—the numbers—in Harlem, with political connections that went right through to the White House. Through his pudgy, uncalloused, overmanicured fingers passed $100,000,000 a year.

Frances ran across the street, breathless, to Martha, and told her the news, in the same emotional exultation that would have possessed a debutante with a sudden invitation from the Prince of Wales.

Martha certainly was not putting her daughter on the market for anybody, but she, too, was swept away with the mighty magnificence of the name. She advised Frances to go for a drive with him in the big, slinky, steel-jacketed and bulletproof car that she could see from her window. Frances, hatless and flushed, ran back and got an hour off. When Dutch Schultz asked, few people questioned.

As she came out, two men slipped from the front seat, and as one opened the door the other, with his hand inside his coat at his armpit where he carried his gat, looked up and down the block. Schultz and Frances got in and the door closed with that authority which only a high-priced limousine can express with a bang and a click.

Within a month, Frances was Mrs. Arthur Flegenheimer. It was infatuation on the whisper of a name, but it had grown into a tremendous and all-conquering love. Few romances with figures that defy the law were ever more mutually fervent and sincere.

Schultz was always in trouble. Despite the enormous sums he took in, he had to pay out, at times, more. He cheated on his Federal and State income taxes, kept enormous staffs of bodyguards and fixers and collectors, and when he wasn't hunted by the Internal Revenue men he was tracked by gunmen of rivals who wanted to take over. He was frequently arrested and numerous times shot at, and his only chance for a few hours or days of happiness with his bride was to drive to remote villages in New England or 100 miles out on Long Island, where, under an assumed name, he might hole in for a day or two before someone recognized him.

Thus they lived for four years, in which time two children were born, first a girl and then a boy. She proudly named their son Arthur Flegenheimer, Jr.

He bathed Frances in furs which she didn't want to wear, and weighed her down with jewels which she rarely wore; and he got her up in the middle of nights and took her to strange places, whence they frequently had to escape on a moment's notice, more than once to the music of whining bullets.

On October 9, 1935, they were under cover in a hotel in Newark, N. J. They dined in their rooms and then he told her he had to meet some of his henchmen in a little restaurant. She went to a movie. Schultz walked into a little café and joined two other men on a bench in a booth.

The two favorite methods of murder among the outlaws were "put him on the spot" and "take him for a ride." The first was designed to plant a victim, drawn by treachery, to be slaughtered by executioners who would know just where and when, and thus elude the uncertainties of pursuit or having to do a job in a public street. The theory of "taking for a ride" also was usually carried out through misplaced faith, though sometimes at the point of a gun, and its strategy lay in taking the body-to-be out to a quiet, lonely spot where there would probably be no police or witnesses.

Dutch Schultz was put on the spot.

No sooner had he sat down than the two men who had lured him there dived to the floor, as a man in a green hat stepped out from behind a pillar and gave Schultz all his six bullets in the belly, the gangster's favorite target. To make certainty doubly sure, he was shot with slugs dipped in garlic, a deadly poison to the mucous membranes of the bowels. They took him in an ambulance to a hospital, where he died raving, with Frances' name on his lips. The first she knew she was a widow was when two detectives closed in on her as she returned to her hotel.

Of course, she had a faint idea of who had done it or who had ordered it done. But she hadn't been Dutch Schultz' wife for four years not to know the penalty for blowing the whistle on the Mafia which had ordered the execution.

From that moment on, she was hounded and hunted by prosecutors who wanted to know who had killed Dutch Schultz; by tax collectors who wanted to know where his money was—those millions he was supposed to have cached; by his former associates, who thought they were entitled to some of the money—and where was it?

She lived as a fugitive for years. She had no money. She knew of no money. She knew that he owned a brewery in Yonkers worth more than a million dollars, but he had never dared put it in his own name and those who now controlled it shrugged their shoulders and said they knew nothing of any interest he had. She went to "Dixie" Davis, his lawyer, whom Schultz had made rich, but he had nothing and knew nothing. She sold her furs and jewels, which supported her and the children for a couple of years.

Then she was flat broke.

She worked as a saleswoman in Bloomingdale's, as a waitress, and almost went blind inspecting minute precision parts in Sperry's. Martha had died in an automobile accident and she was alone with her babies.

Not only were the essentials of living a problem, but being allowed to live was even more perplexing. For a while she refused to haul down her flag. She was Mrs. Arthur Flegenheimer and her son was Arthur Flegenheimer, Jr. But when boardinghouse keepers learned who Arthur Flegenheimer had been, and cruel little boys learned who Arthur Flegenheimer, Jr., was, Frances had to pack the little she had and move.

From rooming house to cheap hotel to boarding-house in New Jersey, Westchester, Long Island villages and the fastnesses of Manhattan tenements, where few give a damn about who lives next door, she fled and fled again as the ghost of Dutch Schultz caught up with her.

Exhausted, penniless, she went back to her church, the church she had left when she married out of her faith.

The priests were kind and understanding. They took the children to a place in the Rocky Mountains and, with the mother's consent, gave them a new last name.

No one out there knew Dutch Schultz; few of the rugged folks had ever heard of him.

Frances followed. She, too, took the name the children had assumed. We must not divulge it.

She turned her back on the city which had given her birth, the city which had given her romance and the city which had booted her around and sneered and pointed in derision to her and her children, the widow and the babies of Dutch Schultz.

She is a nurse in a Catholic hospital, still in her early thirties, still soft and attractive. She loves her new purpose and her new surroundings and the peace and usefulness of her life. Your authors know just where she is and who she is, but they will keep it confidential—even from her old friends on Dream Street—The Canyon!

3. THE MAIN DRAG

IF BROADWAY is a "state of mind," as some phrase inventor put it, a clinical psychiatrist should diagnose it. He might isolate the precise form of dementia which drives this wacky world of fancy, flesh, piracy, pruriency and pure poesy to its multiform objectives.

Nowhere else do the Lord and the Devil work so nearly side by side.

Here romance, misery, murder, adultery, mother-love and human frailty are commodities; carnal appeal and ridicule and horror are inventoried and price-tagged; the money-changers throng the steps of the temples of art with none to castigate them.

Slashing through the very center of traffic in solid substances, this highway of economic parasitism dominates the scene.

* * *

New York is a great seaport—so are Baltimore and Boston; New York is a great factory town—so are Cleveland and Detroit; New York is a great railroad terminal—Chicago is greater; New York is a great seat of learning—so is Los Angeles.

The difference is still Broadway. There is only one!

In its days of richest glory, Broadway's crown jewels were its masters of stage production; their thrones were its theatres where their works reigned.

Of all these, not even excepting the brothers Frohman, the most lustrous was David Belasco. He covered

16

a wider range of time as well as of topic. He was the archdirector, a playwright of cunning talent, a manager and star maker. He was a more intensely exciting character than any he ever dreamed up.

He built the Belasco Theatre, which was his showcase, his workshop, his royal castle, his private museum, and his play pen.

Past 76, he was vigorous, virile, and planning for the future.

Mr. B. (even his mistresses called him that) told one of your authors, who was his intimate friend despite a wide disparity in ages, that he couldn't truly interest himself in a play unless he had a sweetheart in the cast.

Handsome, distinguished, with hypnotic and penetrating eyes under black lashes in contrast with snow-white hair, wearing always a priestlike costume which he had designed and would never explain, his years did not dim the electric effect he exercised on beautiful women.

Six floors above street level, over the stage flies of the Belasco, he had fitted up a private gallery housing the spoils of the ages—tapestries, paintings, rare furniture, Venetian glass, armor, snuffboxes, statues, miscellany.

Beside it was a complete living suite, practical but furnished with antique plunder. There he often lived while in the pangs and ecstasies of conception, preparation, and consummation of his plays. Few ever penetrated that sanctum.

He had another private retreat on the balcony level, walled in off the nave. There he received esoterically but with broad hospitality, with a steward to serve drinks and tidbits.

In that room, one night, while a hit play was in action below, he got word from his stage manager that a feminine principal had fluffed some lines. He sent for her after the act. In the presence of one of your authors, he berated her as a gold-bricker and an ingrate.

"I gave you everything you ever had," he shrilled. "And the first thing I ever gave you was a bath!"

She bitched up no lines in the next act.

The next season another beauty gave him the romantic interest he required for a later success.

At the height of its run, he was stricken with pneumonia. His amazing constitution and will licked it, though he had passed his 76th birthday.

Weakened as the great Belasco was, the soul of the great lover still burned within him. He had been in retirement for weeks. The girl, a blonde this time, was young, and, he feared, fickle. As long as he was on his feet, none of his mistresses dared stray around. But he had been laid up for weeks.

The inamorata of the moment was ensconced in a private three-story residence not far from the Gladstone Hotel where he lived. Because of his family she could not come to see him during his illness. He did not tell her when he would be allowed out again. And, the first night he could ambulate, he decided to spy on her.

He set up his post across the street, where, from behind a light-pole, he could look up and over.

A sudden rainstorm poured out of the sky, and with

it a cold wind. But he had seen a shadow—of a man and woman, it seemed to him. And with the consuming zeal and drive with which he did everything, he remained there, drenched and shivering, ignoring everything but those windows.

He found out nothing.

But the exposure resulted in a second attack of pneumonia.

That tawdry anticlimax ended the life of the genius at whose feet Broadway had bowed—a martyr to suicidal jealousy at his advanced age—jealousy over a run-of-the-mill gal whose name no one would remember on the street that will never forget him.

a.—*Give My Regards to Broadway*

When Georgie Cohan penned his crude classic, New York's Main Drag ran from Herald Square at 34th Street, on Broadway, to Times Square at 43rd Street, with tentacles precariously reaching northward a few blocks and a few outposts of the Tenderloin's last frontiers stretching southward.

Broadway's uptown growth had been progressive from historic days when the theatre and hotel zones were around City Hall Park, not far from the Battery.

During the years, successively, Diamond Ditch moved up, centering at 14th Street, then again at 23rd Street, coming to anchor at Herald Square before its final migration to Times Square.

Within memory of men who for old time's sake are still called "middle-aged," the crest of the White Way was in the 30's. Here such noted playhouses as the Herald Square, Garrick, Empire and Casino had clustered about them the town's half-a-hundred legit theatres. The still standing and thriving Metropolitan Opera House was then the Mecca of Pittsburgh millionaires.

On Broadway, in the district and its side streets, were famous cabarets and night clubs, places like the Normandie, the Pre-Cat, Café l'Opera and others.

The tide imperceptibly but inevitably flowed northward. Even while Herald Square was in its ascendancy, Times Square bloomed and blossomed, with 42nd Street, between Broadway and Eighth Avenue, flashing more legitimate theatres than any other block in the world.

By the end of World War I, Gay Gulch had crossed the great divide, was almost entirely north of 42nd Street, though many theatres and a few night clubs continued to stay below 42nd Street as late as the early 20's.

The coming of Prohibition found most of Gotham's glamor studding what we still call the White Way.

The Paramount Theatre now occupies the site of Shanley's famed café. The Claridge, popular-priced tourist hangout, was originally Rector's and later, as the Claridge, top spot for stage and movie names.

The Knickerbocker Hotel, with its memorable bar and the Parrish painting of King Cole, was at 42nd and Broadway. Today it is the *Newsweek* Building. The King Cole painting now hangs in the aristocratic bar of the St. Regis Hotel on Fifth Avenue.

The Palais Royale operated in the present location of the Latin Quarter, at 48th; the New York Roof was atop a structure on the site now occupied by the new Criterion Theatre; the Bartholdi Inn, celebrated theatrical boardinghouse, was at 46th and Broadway, where Loew's State now stands.

The coming of Prohibition dispersed the pickle factories. The big places with grand old names couldn't stand up without liquor revenue. The wining and dining industry was taken over by a new breed and operated in side street cellars and stables and old residences.

At the same time, a number of new night clubs, mostly intimate affairs, were opened on Broadway. These were not supposed to be speaks. You brought your own makin's and they supplied the set-ups. If you forgot your flask and they knew you, they'd get you all you could carry.

The most celebrated speakeasies were clustered in every side street of the 40's and 50's on both sides of Broadway, and down to the East River.

Some of the most famous night clubs of the present period such as the Stork Club and Leon & Eddie's began as humble blind tigers. More about them in later chapters.

Among the rooms best remembered from the torrid 20's are the El Fey, Tex Guinan's, the Madrid, the Hotsy Totsy, the Abbey, the Silver Slipper, the Plantation, the Argonaut, the Frivolities, La Sportiva, Cap Williams', the 50-50 Club, and Sid Solomon's Central Park Casino, which was Jimmy Walker's night "City Hall."

Some had lurid histories, with gangland killings and knifings an almost everyday commonplace. But many of today's Hollywood and Broadway greats came out of this hurly-burly.

Harry Richman and Morton Downey both played pianos in speaks.

Georgie Raft hoofed at Roseland dance hall, later for Tex Guinan, at $50 a week.

Joan Crawford, then Lucille Le Seur, worked as a show gal at the Frivolities, where a fabulous story of Cinderella on the Main Stem happened.

* * *

It was the custom on Sunday nights to hold chorus girl "opportunity contests," at which outstanding youngsters appeared and sang or danced.

The winner was awarded a $50 bill.

These contests were conducted by Nils T. Granlund, a character truly as fantastic as the lies told about him, who had been Marcus Loew's personal press agent and the first radio star in the country, working under the pseudonymic initials, N.T.G. He became the leading café man of his age.

N.T.G., known as "Granny" to thousands in show business, was then directing the entertainment policy of the Frivolities, as well as ten other midtown clubs, and the "opportunity contests" were rotated from club to club, week after week.

Tests of this sort, run on the level, can become tremendously dreary affairs. So Granny picked out three sparklers from as many shows and arranged for them to enter all the contests.

One of his trio always won.

One of these pert pigeons was a show gal named Ruby Stevens. Today, in Hollywood, she's known as Barbara Stanwyck.

Another was Clare Luce—the actress, not the playwright-politician.

The third was Lucilla Mendez, who became an exotic star.

One Sunday night, back in the 20's, the contest was at the Frivolities.

At the appointed time, each of the three took the floor and did her little song or dance. They were so good, having it down pat by now, that they expected no competition from uninitiated outsiders.

But one dared it, an unknown child who looked about 13. Compared to the three sleek and sexy sirens who had preceded her, she was bedraggled. Her heels were worn down, her stockings in runs and her face shiny.

The audience tittered. But she stole their hearts with a brand of dancing never before seen on jaded Gaiety Gulch.

The customers cheered. They shouted. They screamed.

So, though the three hot-house lovelies sneered and pouted, Granny handed the youngster the prize. And he told her he was going to put her to work at the Strand Roof, at $50 a week. The girl almost fainted.

As an afterthought, N.T.G. asked her name.

She replied: "Ruby Keeler."

She became that almost mythical creation, "The Toast of Broadway."

She was taken under the "wing" of Johnny Irish, a long since forgotten gangster, whose hoodlums saw to it no others romanced her. But Al Jolson, then the king of show business, fell—and hard. Irish, who loved her with a love that passeth understanding, called the singer to his hotel room. Al, fearing he was about to be taken for a ride, was agreeably surprised when the mobster asked what "his intentions are."

In relief, Al blurted out that he wanted to marry the dancer. Big-hearted Irish adopted a noble pose, gave the girl up.

"I'll take my boys to Atlantic City," he said, "and you hop an ocean liner with Ruby. Otherwise maybe some of them will get an idea you're taking her away from me and maybe they won't like it. And heaven help you if you don't marry her."

She married Al Jolson at 17. She hit film stardom. Then she chucked it, still in her twenties, to marry a poor boy, rusticate in Pasadena and have four children.

b.—*No Cover Charge*

By 1928, it seemed Prohibition was here to stay. The easy money boys, grown fat and rich with two-by-four hideaway speaks, began to think about expanding.

But when a law-evading night club got too big, too noisy, too public, even the usually complaisant cops had to smack it down. And if they didn't, a rival mob did.

The hotel grills and roofs, forced to go straight to protect huge investments, long were dead ducks by now and so were the hotels. There just was no big place where a man and girl could go and have some dancing and fun, unless he was known to the gorilla at the door and could afford citrate of magnesia labeled Mumm's at $35 a throw.

That year, Granlund had a vision.

He conceived the idea of building a huge cabaret room, large enough to pay off on quantity business alone, instead of bootlegging.

As a further inducement to lure the wary man of moderate means, ducking high prices, fancy foreign headwaiters and tremendous tariffs, he invented the minimum charge, to supplant the imported and resented couvert.

A syndicate built such a cabaret on Broadway, between 48th and 49th Streets, in a room once occupied by Rector's of hallowed memory, and after that having housed a chop suey palace.

The new place was named the Hollywood Restaurant. It got off to an immediate success with big bands, famous acts, and the most beautiful girls this side of heaven.

The great Ziegfeld, as a smart business, tied up with N.T.G. on an exchange policy, which called for a selected few of the Hollywood girls to double into the "Follies," an equal number of the glorified doubling into the Hollywood.

No liquor was sneaked at the club, but if you brought your own you were sold a set-up (costing two cents) for a buck.

The Hollywood's success was immediate, and before

the club expired more than a decade later, it had lived to see the cover charge die.

Club after club in New York, Chicago, Hollywood, Europe, Asia, South America, followed the policy of elaborate shows and minimum charge. The Hollywood was the daddy of practically every cabaret in business today.

This revolution, plus the hard times following 1929, again changed the face of Rue de Revelry and environs. Even before Repeal, many clubs of the Guinan era and stamp folded, including Guinan's. On one side, they were hammered by the depression; on the other they were against the competition offered by the Hollywood and its imitators.

A new crop of lovelies had come up, were displayed and went on to Hollywood. To mention one, Alice Faye—a Hollywood Restaurant pony.

Rudy Vallee, leading the band there, adopted her as a protégée. He later took her with him into George White's *Scandals,* in which he starred.

Alice, who had dark brown hair in those pre-blonde days, did one bit number. It was enough, with Rudy's backing, to show trained talent scouts.

Soon came the equally large and elaborate Paradise Restaurant, across Broadway from the Hollywood, to compete. The syndicate which built it lured N.T.G. away from the Hollywood, some said at the point of a gun. There were times during those shimmering nights when show girls, those with followings, were paid as much as $250 a week simply to undulate across the floor. Many were driven to work in Rolls-Royces.

Minks—even sables—were a dime a dozen. Naked was the doll whose arms weren't covered with diamond bracelets.

Fifteen years ago, the hegira to the East Side had not gotten under way. Playboys, head salesmen, mobsters, visiting firemen—all fast with a buck—nightly made happy the hearts of headwaiters.

c.—*From the Circle to the Square*

Though what the world calls "Broadway" is not a street, but a condition, the purpose of these few pages is to tell you about the thoroughfare named Broadway, and more specifically, that part of it now the Rialto of the western world.

This meandering bit of avenue, following the tortuous curve of an ancient cow path, is delimited south of 42nd Street by the flourishing wholesale garment industry; and, north of Columbus Circle, by Central Park and automobile row, some of which extends south of the Circle, encroaching into the White Way as far as 54th Street. So, all the Glittering Gash can honestly claim for its own is 12 short blocks, measuring exactly three-fifths of a mile.

This is the street of a million lights, of a broken heart for every bulb, and more bulbs every night.

This is Gotham's Main Drag; strangely, save for the milling crowds and the blinding Mazdas, it has not now and has not had for the past decade those features which are universally supposed by all the people "in the know" all over the world, except in New York, to be on Broadway.

At this writing, on the whole "street," there are but two theatres permanently devoted to the legitimate stage.

But there are more than 30 legitimate theatres in New York. All, except the aforementioned and a handful on parallel avenues, are located east and west of Broadway, in narrow side streets in the 40's and 50's.

Of about 1,500 licensed cabarets in New York, there are at this writing but four with entrances on the Stem.

If, from seeing the film of that name, you thought 42nd Street—where is crosses Broadway—is the center of Manhattan's mad gaiety, you have much to learn.

That thoroughfare, once the home of a dozen proud theatres including the New Amsterdam of red plush and wonderful memories, is now devoted exclusively to "grind" movie houses, penny arcades, flea circuses, army and navy goods stores, orange juice stands and frowzy but friendly dames.

Broadway teems with dime dance halls, open air hot dog counters, photo and shooting galleries, souvenir and novelty holes-in-the-wall. It is the honky-tonk that was Coney Island, the crossroads carnival.

But, strangely enough, in the daytime, when the bright lights that draw the rubes are off and Broadway's sidewalks are comparatively free, it reverts to its old estate as the home and capital of the entertainment world.

For here, and nearby, are the offices of the theatrical producers, the agents who sell the acts, the dance studios where embryo chorus fillies learn to hoof; the costumers and the booters, the scenic artists and designers—and Tin Pan Alley.

* * *

When Mike Jacobs moved his handmade teeth and his principality of pugs a few feet west to Madison Square Garden, he broke up a mongrel marriage of sock and song, which had long been the Brill Building.

An old-fashioned, ten-story structure, smoke-grimed, with creaking and groaning elevators, it had become the stronghold and nerve center of two giant industries.

Prize-fighters, the tycoons and tramps who manage them, rubbers, sponge-carriers, trainers and the motley mob which gathers around the boxing racket rubbed against music publishers, composers, lyric writers, piano players, arrangers and the others of the equally heterogeneous individuals engaged in creating and selling the songs of the world.

On the main floor, facing Broadway, are two cafés—the Turf, hangout for musicians, and Dempsey's, rendezvous of pugs.

Across the street, on the 49th Street side, is the Forrest Hotel, long the secondary concentration headquarters for the boys of Jacobs' Beach. Up the street and across Eighth Avenue is the Garden, the Taj Mahal of the biff business.

In the dingy Brill Building, day and night, swarm the unsung individuals of the singing empire, in every respect unique and little known outside its own realm.

There are 320 firms in New York City that publish

music. Of these a dozen are highly successful, another half dozen do well and the rest are mostly shoestring affairs, picking up the ragged edges and discards of the leaders.

The *sine qua non* of a music publisher is his demonstrating rooms. These are usually tiny cubicles scarcely larger than the battered upright pianos they contain, each manned by a key-thumper who can transpose, ad lib and torture a melody into any tempo for any purpose from a soft-shoe dance accompaniment to a cry for help that would break your heart.

Getting these songs before the public, or as the trade terms it, the "plug," is perhaps the soul of the industry. There are scores of men and women infesting every radio station and theatre where "flesh" performances still remain. Their business is to get their songs sung or played or whistled or even ground out on a hand organ. The big stars are hard to approach and the business, which is organized, has long ago put a foot down on what was formerly an elaborate system of bribery, so that personality, pleading, pull, as often as actual merit and fitness, go to place songs with leading orchestras and ace headliners.

But a late development in the business, one which suspiciously smacks of a restraint of trade violation, is the practice of some publishers of giving a stock interest in their firms to noted crooners, band leaders and disk jockeys, who in return "plug" the latest publications of the companies in which they are interested.

An offshoot of this kind of tie-up, which has the further effect of keeping the compositions of the unknown or the unelect from the market, is off-the-record agreements between the principal publishing houses tied up with singers and band leaders to play only the product of the companies in the charmed circle. You scratch my back and I'll scratch yours.

The demonstrating offices are besieged by ambitious youngsters, failures and never-could-be's who think that they can find a "Yes, We Have No Bananas" or "Smoke Gets in Your Eyes" to draw them to the top overnight. These are inconsequential persons and they are insulted and refused, but they break through here and there.

For a bad singer, all songs are bad. Yet it is in the nature of the stage-struck never to admit that they have failed, but to carry the deathless conviction that it is the "material." They haunt the music publishers, fighting for a chance at the latest, always with high expectations that this time this will be it.

So the Brill Building, overrun as it was for years with every element of the prize ring and the sheet music world and its vocalists and hoofers and bandsmen, naturally became a beehive for minor agents, who pick up shabby fees from unimportant performers.

Some of these have offices in telephone booths and some of them only in their hats. For a commission they will try to sell anything to anybody. They watch the cheap saloons for a "disappointment"—which means that an act has fallen out temporarily or permanently because of delirium tremens, dismissal or death; they try to induce other saloons, without entertainers, to try some—find small, off-key dens and seek to sell them a singer or a sister act. The amount of aggressiveness and persistence they put into their misspent endeavors would probably get them a good income anywhere else—but they would be out of "show business," and they never will be.

Tin Pan Alley has its own glossary. All songs are "numbers." Love songs, mother songs, anything romantic, are "ballads"—a remote adaptation of the original word. All songs of regret and revenge and love's bitter grief are "torches." All crazy songs, which make no sense, are "freaks." All crazy songs which make some sense are "novelties." War songs are "flag wavers." All songs about the south are "Dixies."

The overnight possibilities of radio and millions of juke-box and parlor records have revolutionized the arts and wiles and guiles of "plugging," which is too bad in some ways, though the members of the craft were generally about as venal vultures as the morasses of Manhattan have disgorged.

Their vocation gave them license to knock on dressing-room doors, and many pressed their advantage beyond the call of duty.

They had expense accounts, some professional standing and a fund of that gutter shrewdness and knowledge which are perilous possessions of the unprincipled, yet licensed, scavengers who infest the outer rims of a world which holds forth a few miraculous rewards and an untold number of sordid soul-searings to young, impressionable, overoptimistic girls who reach so desperately for that one chance in a million.

Such girls are exposed to contacts in getting costumes, make-up, dancing shoes, printed "notices," their very jobs. They are hectic, striving, not subject to the reactions and restraints of sheltered, normal living.

And it is no attack on the geniuses and executives of the music business to state that the riffraff of its ragtag has a sustained record of abusing the hospitality of a harum-scarum world where shadow and substance have undefined borders.

* * *

Nearby, too, are the home offices of all the giant Hollywood studios. The pavements, which at night echo and re-echo to the tread of millions of heels, are pre-empted all day by cigar-smoking, side-of-mouth-talking, sure-thing artists and wise boys; bookies, promoters, pluggers, gamblers, hangers-on and layers-off.

The southeast corner of 50th Street and Seventh Avenue epitomizes the decline of the Stem. Gone is the glamorous Earl Carroll Theatre that once graced the spot.

Today, where the most beautiful girls in the world passed through the magic portals, there is a two-story taxpayer with a five-and-dime, a chain pharmacy and a chop suey emporium.

The career of Earl Carroll was as fantastic as any in show business. A Pittsburgh theatre usher turned flyer in the embryo air force of World War I, Earl first made his mark as a song writer, when Enrico Caruso bought special lyrics from him.

Even before he built the first of his two theatres, he was pressing Ziegfeld in the girl-show industry.

Yet the trade knows that none of Earl's proud productions ever showed a profit on the books, save *White Cargo,* which wasn't a musical, and the rights to which were taken from him. Carroll, however, lived like a king, on salaries and royalties, though his backers committed suicide, went bankrupt, or both.

On Broadway they still talk of Joyce Hawley's champagne bath. Carroll threw a private party on his stage for friends and backers. Miss Hawley, teen-age chorine, was ordered to bathe in a tub of champagne. Some said she was nude.

Carroll was indicted—not because Joyce wore nothing, but because he denied he bought the wine. Earl was true to his bootlegger, claimed it was only ginger ale. So he did a bit in Atlanta for perjury, rather than blow the whistle.

Carroll's second theatre opened in 1931, with the eleventh edition of the "Vanities." It was the most magnificent legit house ever built, with luxuriously decorated rest rooms for the chorines and a backstage that could play a circus. Before the year was out, they took the house away from him. The $5,000,000 structure limped along as a cinema revival house and cabaret, only to be razed for a Woolworth.

Washed up with New York, Earl produced a supperclub floor show at Palm Island Casino, Miami, in 1935, and again in 1936, when the intrenched mobsters kicked him out. Carroll moved on to Hollywood.

Half the movie colony came in as stockholders on his first night club, the idea being that they would own special private boxes. But the financing came to a halt when the framework was up. The stockholders bowed out and Earl got control. His success in Hollywood became legendary; he lived like an Eastern potentate in a mansion that made a movie set look like a Quonset shanty.

Plenty happened on and off Broadway—to the Earl of Carroll!

*   *   *

The complexion changes at dinnertime, when the excursionists and suburbanites, disgorged by the train-loads from subway kiosks, take over.

The rush reaches its peak between 8 and 8:30, when the steady but slow-moving stream of stragglers, strollers and starers meets the head-on rush of theatre-bound hordes.

Again at 11, when the curtains fall in three dozen houses, there is a mad scramble of hemmed-in humanity.

Soon after midnight, though the lights still blink bravely, the crowd thins out and drops off. Broadway, having lost most of the places that attract revelers, is no longer a late street.

Its larger night clubs, patronized more by tourists and middle-class burghers, have little play after 2 A.M. Only a few even bother to present late shows, though in other sections of the city floor entertainment runs until 4 o'clock.

When the gawkers get off the Stem—but long before the break of day—it is taken over by its third set of citizens.

Dope-peddlers work the west side of the street, between 45th and 47th Streets, and on Seventh Avenue, between 48th and 50th Streets, on the east side of the street.

You can buy reefers in a dozen cheap bars on 48th between Sixth and Seventh Avenues, and at 51st and Seventh, in front of the cafeteria. In fact, when Federal agents haven't their full quota of pinches in at the end of the month, they tap people at random here—and almost every one has the "makings."

Blowzy hookers congregate at 47th.

Runners for clip joints work outside the bigger bars and clubs. Policy pay-off men visit the saloons and cigar stands.

About this time, too, chorines and musicians are getting off. They swarm into the sandwich bars, delicatessens, lunch counters and all-night drugstore fountains.

The first faint streaks of dawn, breaking through the long, narrow lanes to light now almost deserted Broadway, point the way home to offside hotels and bed for make-up-streaked cuties who may dream of Hollywood, fame and fortune.

And this year, and next year, and every year, maybe five will find it.

The pages immediately preceding and following this chapter are devoted to those portions of the New York scene which, not physically on the street known as Broadway, are so intimately connected with it that in the idiom of the city they are referred to as "Broadway."

For instance, "Dream Street," the theatre section, and 52nd Street's Swing Lane are parts of the Broadway scene, though the latter is a good 300 yards removed from the Stem.

At this writing, the late Mayor LaGuardia's verboten on the old institution of burlesque still stands, but the average peasant will not be looking for it here, because his own home town probably tolerates at least one burly-Q house.

The nearest theatres dispensing that form of entertainment are in Union City, N. J., reached by Lincoln Tunnel, or 42nd Street ferry (10 minutes) and in Newark, reached by Hudson Tube (30 minutes) or Pennsylvania Railroad (15 minutes).

Though the so-called "Poor Man's Musical Comedy" is outlawed here, many of our $5 and $6 musicals and stage plays contain material that would make the most frenzied front-row burlesque patron blush. But there are still no "strippers."

One gal of our acquaintance who had made a respectable and comfortable living on the road (even in Boston) peeling in night clubs and theatres, was booked into one of our larger cafés last year.

Aware of the police ban on that form of art, she revised her act to a comedy strip-tease, which left her clothed almost as completely as an Eskimo maiden, at the crucial end of the bit.

But, next day, the management got one word from the cops—"Nix!" The monitors of modesty admitted the girl was completely clad. "But," said they, "it is a sub for a strip-tease."

There is nothing approaching the nudity permitted in other cities in our midtown clubs.

Navels must be covered.

As for higher up—

If you have tears, prepare to shed them now. That's about all you can still shed on Broadway.

4. THE THEATAH!

THOUGH FILMS, radio, video and even night clubs far surpass the legit in numbers of those employed and in earnings of most stars, New York is the last citadel on this continent of that phantasmagoria of the ages, the theatre.

Shubert Alley, a narrow private street running from 44th to 45th, behind the Astor Hotel, is its ventricle. Within a 300-foot radius are some of the most important playhouses, the thrones of most of the theatrical impresarios and mighty agents, and the dining places and haunts of the distinctive, generic folk who compose this gregarious galaxy. Old-timers, and some stars, still foregather in the Astor Hunting Room. The mart and meeting place for lunch, dinner and after openings is Sardi's.

The youngsters eat at Walgreen's drugstore, 44th Street and Broadway, and the drugstore in the Astor; instead of cocktails they sip cokes and smoke reefers.

Here they swap dreams, inveigh against the "favoritism" that holds them back and tell what they'd do if they had the part instead of Helen Hayes.

Unfortunately, too many of the adolescents have been tinged with political radicalism and tainted with homosexuality.

Yet, the New York theatre is still the most vital and vibrant facet of show business, and from it comes almost everything good in its bastard offspring, radio, its newer brother, television, and the movies.

Despite the thousands of accounts that have been written about the drama, the comedy and the cruelty that go into an offering in a first-class playhouse, no one has yet conveyed realistically the hopes, the fears, the prayers, of the actors, the authors, the directors, producers and attachés as they approach and experience the momentous opening night.

It is a gigantic gamble, forever in untried walks; for the over-all combination is never the same.

One chuckle in the right spot can make a career and a million dollars; a dimple in a knee, an ad lib side remark which is left in because it was spontaneous, an expression on one face at a critical moment, have been known to do it. Yet, no one has ever lived who could say, before an audience has put thumbs up or down, "This is a hit."

There has been much controversy over the power of the critics. In New York, these dozen professional reviewers are a jury, voting the fate of many men and women, who are on the defensive. But there is no presumption of innocence, and there are no attorneys to plead for the accused.

There is the right of appeal, to the public; and, once in a miracle moon, the people override the reviewers.

Saddle-sore, jaded, blasé playgoers they are; honest, usually. Broadway-wise, they can recognize a success. Because they are regulars and show-weary, they are quickest to rise to anything above mediocrity.

Having been critics, we know the way the fellows

react and feel. They are not vicious deliberately, as many have charged; nor are they soft and sympathetic, as many would have them. They have a job to do and their obligation is to the reader, not to the subjects of their criticism.

The first-nighter, whose mass response in a measure prompts and primes the critics, is likewise a recidivist, an addict, and therefore a tough customer. He and she make all the openings—to see, usually to sneer, sometimes to cheer, often to be sadistically delighted at the spectacle of a misspent endeavor.

They do not go, like others, because they are especially drawn by a star or a playwright or the glamor of a title, or—which is most important—because they have heard or read that this is worth seeing. Those who do so are in the mood to be pleased. Those who go to show off sables and necklaces, to see how others dress, to brush against the wise crowd and gossip in the intermissions, are, at the very best, neutral.

And they grow impatient and belligerent because too many around them are synthetically enthusiastic.

Those would be the husbands, wives, sweeties, neighbors, creditors and kin of everyone affected by the life-and-death trial. They laugh on hair-triggers, applaud bit-players' entrances, loudly approve.

They are no corporal's guard. In a city like this, there are a half-million people directly concerned in the destinies of the theatre.

The average company includes 20 performers, 13 stagehands, a unit manager, a press agent, from one to three authors, a director and assistant director, often an orchestra, as often a chorus of 12 to 40, not to mention the house employees. Hundreds have worked on costumes, painting and constructing scenery, the properties (movable tangibles), advertising, wigmaking, lighting, photographing and the many other processes that go into something that someone "presents."

None of these persons must miss a première. Seldom is a single ticket bought, so multiply automatically by two. Then add collateral and congenital kin and romantic close ones.

These favorably prejudiced rooters, plus the asbestos-lined, never-miss first-nighters, plus the critics, the hawk-eyed scalpers, the hard-boiled New York scouts for Hollywood, the agents of the players or acquisitive agents looking for clients, nervous stockholders in the theatre and show and their staffs, comprise the hundreds "out front" on the monumental night when everything is riding on an uncharted path toward a gold mine or a morass.

It is not a "representative" audience. But it represents New York and all the 48 States. For this is the night of decision!

There has been much talk and squawk for "constructive criticism." It would mean about nothing. By the time is appears, it would have to be reconstructive. And it's then too late.

A handful of plays have upset the original opinion, notably *Abie's Irish Rose, Tobacco Road* and *Hellzapoppin'*. In all those instances, and the few others where a production caught its second wind, the backers were game and optimistic, plowed through losses with a confidence rare in such enterprises.

As a rule, what the first-nighters say as they come out is final, be it an Ibsen revival or a Theatre Guild musical or a bawdy revue.

Word spreads amazingly fast and far. Fifteen minutes after a smash has rung down, the cigar-store crowds in the Bronx and the burghers on Staten Island and the stoop-sitters in far Flatbush are chewing about it. For a big hit is big business in the Big Burg.

No recurrent event, including contest sports, sells papers like an important opening. Thousands know that what the critics say means a flop or a run. Not only are many directly interested, but millions follow such news, as Los Angeles reads Hollywood trade matter, Chicago goes for stockyards' statistics, Detroit watches auto output, Washington eats up politics and Memphis seeks the latest on "the state of the River."

For the stage is a colossal industry in Greater New York.

Its "legitimate" houses turn over more than $1,000,-000 a week in good months.

Its unions are rich and powerful, its personnel exceeds in volume the population of some metropolitan cities.

Yet its fortunes hang on invisible, intangible hairs!

5. SWING LANE

IN DEFIANCE of police regulations, two lines of sleek and fancy limousines are parked nightly outside Jack and Charlie's famed 21 Club in 52nd Street.

One reason why the cops close their eyes while pounding that beat is that the cars, with liveried chauffeurs, are owned by the rich and prominent townsfolk. Another is that many of the machines carry burnished seals, signifying they belong to, or at least are assigned to, high city, state and national officials.

West of Fifth Avenue, 52nd Street was long a street of wealth. Today, the 21 Club is wealth's last outpost.

This was a baronial thoroughfare, lined on both sides by fancy brownstone and brick residences of solid and superior citizens.

But the northward encroachment of business, culminating in the late 20's and early 30's with the construction of Rockefeller Center only a block south, drove the householders elsewhere.

Many of the luxurious brownstones were converted into rooming houses and made over into one- and two-room apartments; but the chief industry in the block was speakeasies. The street was a natural—it ran in the right direction, i.e., its one-way traffic was routed from west to east, which in midtown New York is important, because the bulk and the best of aftertheatre traffic goes that way.

Repeal brought new problems. Drinkers wanted

43

more room and more air. A dozen years of small, smoky dives caused claustrophobia.

In 1933, they welcomed the big, roomy, hotel grills and Broadway cafés.

Of the 50-odd blind pigs in 52nd Street, between Fifth and Sixth, only two remained. But those two have become national institutions.

By far the most famous cabaret night club in the country is Leon & Eddie's, at 33 West 52nd Street. It started in 1929 as a narrow, dingy speak, directly across the street from its present premises, at No. 18, now part of Rockefeller Center.

The 21 Club, next door to Leon & Eddie's, technically is a restaurant, not a night club, inasmuch as only food and liquor are served; no show or music.

A history of the 21 parallels the decline of society, about which more in a succeeding chapter.

Its proprietors, former speakeasy operators, came to be considered arbiters of high fashion. It was supposed to be a great honor to be permitted to enter their saloon. And if one of the bosses deigned to talk to you, it was regarded by many as equal to being a box-holder at the Metropolitan Opera.

When one of them (Jack Kriendler) got scorched in the papers, however, it was over a mess with a middle-aged Long Island matron, and the whole town howled with the anticlimax of it all. Kriendler died at the early age of 48. His funeral, attended by top names, was the social event of the season.

Though most of 52nd Street's gin joints folded and

died in 1933, the thoroughfare did not lose its essential
character as an entertainment avenue.

People were used to it, the traffic advantages remained, and it was near to the Music Hall, Broadway
and the East Side.

Many of the undercover locations blossomed out
under new management, and with new decorations, as
intimate night clubs.

Leon & Eddie's already had moved across the street
and already was famous.

But in a little room, over near Sixth Avenue, called
the Onyx, something happened that set the street for
all time to come.

The Onyx was a musicians' hangout. It seated about
50, specialized in hot licks played by a small pick-up
band, headed by two nimble lads named Farley and
Riley.

They had written a gag song called "The Music
Goes Round and Round." It was unpublished, but by
request they played it eight or ten times a night at the
Onyx, and many of the musicians who came in to relax
joined in the jam sessions and played it with them.

The song was finally published and became one of
the top freaks of all times. Its chief result, however,
was to firmly establish 52nd Street as Swing Lane.

Through the years since then, dozens of clubs have
come and gone on the street, with Leon & Eddie's and
21 the only prominent ones to remain through it all.
Yet it's still known as Swing Lane.

During the past few years its complexion has been

changing, as more and more smaller swing spots have begun to specialize in Negro entertainers and bands.

Many of these small clubs have become, for all practical purposes, "black and tan" spots where whites and Negroes (of opposite sexes) mix, not furtively.

Two other developments in the street—said to be natural consequences of its jazz madness—are the presence of reefer (marijuana) addicts and homosexuals, of all races.

Mind you, these people do not go to Leon & Eddie's or many other places in the block.

But the owners of the clubs they infest—mostly small places near Sixth Avenue—have been helpless before the horde and many of them welcomed this new business.

It is the observation of these writers that mad modern music, sex perversions and narcotic addiction run arm in arm. They surely do in night clubs.

Police and Federals have frequently raided these dumps and arrested dope-peddlers, including musicians, hat-check gals and waiters.

A few of the clubs had their licenses lifted for short periods, but in every instance, when the proprietor proved he didn't know about the lawbreakers, they were restored.

One corner of 52nd and Sixth Avenue is particularly obnoxious, a hangout for prostitutes and homos, dark and light.

But don't let this scare you from a trip to 52nd Street. It is part of the spice, and you are completely safe, especially at Leon & Eddie's.

46

Since V-J Day, many night clubs on the south side of 52nd Street have been torn down to make way for the Standard Oil Building extension of Rockefeller Center.

Many established cabarets were forced to shutter or move when the work first got under way, and present indications are that, before long, the seamier sides of Swing Lane will have disappeared, leaving only a handful of top respectable spots.

Meanwhile, a peculiar situation developed as a result of this infringement by big business. At the eastern end of this one block are stone skyscrapers and exclusive shops showing luxurious wares.

One square to the south is Radio City, and a block north is dignified, restricted 53d Street.

Those who own the real estate at the west end of Swing Lane have a feeling they are directly in the path of Manifest Destiny. Their property has possibilities of incalculable wealth. The golden lightning is scheduled to strike so soon, the freeholders do nothing toward improving the brownstones which still remain, but rent them out at high rates to night clubs on the ground floor while the upper stories cater to transient roomers or have been reconverted into small kitchenette apartments.

In this little valley less than a hundred yards long is a unique concentration of vice and hokum. Here are deadfalls designed especially to attract the tourists with promises of naughty displays of undraped female cuticle; yet, by the time the customer has paid his tab, he's seen nothing more revealing than a fat female sup-

47

posed to be "nude," whose generously proportioned panties and bra (which always remain on) are constructed of material as thick as carpeting, and as opaque.

Yet other places, next door, cater to dope addicts, perverts and streetwalkers, while many of the furnished rooms over some of the most respectable places are frequently employed as assignation houses, or provide drop-ins for youths and young girls seeking places in which to engage in mad marijuana revels.

Fifty-Second Street, between Sixth and Seventh Avenues, has long been the poor sister of Swing Lane, for most of its length a dreary, dingy path of parking lots, garages, closed stables, and a few saloons, though right near Seventh Avenue there are a few first-class restaurants.

Another 52nd Street phenomenon is an influx of Chinese restaurants in the past few years. There are five in a half block off Broadway, and more than a dozen others within a block radius. But more about the uptown Orient in a later chapter.

6. EAST SIDE, BEST SIDE

THE LINES of the Kipling poem have been rewritten. Here we say—"Take me somewhere east of Fifth, where a man can rinse a thirst."

The past decade has seen most of midtown New York's night life—the publicized part, anyway—transferred there.

Here are the places where Gotham's cabaret-wise go; the big glitter and glamor joints on the West Side are for visitors only.

However, when the oaf searches for the so-called entertainment district on the East Side, he will not find it. All the patronage is taxi trade—or drop-ins—from the huge neighboring hotels and apartment buildings. There is no East Side Bright Belt.

The East Side is where you find such snooty places as the Stork Club, El Morocco and the Colony; such gay spots as the Copacabana and the Versailles.

Many of the world's finest and most celebrated dining spots snuggle in the section; there are so many, it would be impossible to give even a sketchy list here. One—Chambord—surrounded by tenements and low groggeries, where pheasant breast sells for $16, is regarded the costliest on earth.

Once the term "East Side" connoted poverty. It signified endless miles of filthy streets, lined with rickety tenements in which millions of Europe's dispossessed struggled for a foothold in the land of promise.

49

Of that East Side—the lower East Side—much remains.

Our present excursus deals only with a wonderland of wealth, a unique Mecca of marble and steel with all the world's riches, that lies above 42nd Street, a creation of recent times—a development in the wake of the electrification of the New York Central tracks, and the opening up of miles of priceless and convenient midtown property to exploitation for residences and office buildings.

This East Side cannot be described in one sentence, nor in one book. It is a Manhattan mélange of money and beauty, prodigality and banality, with haunts and hangouts of every description, from pizzerias for truckdrivers to regal retreats.

There is the world-famed Stork, owned by the *sui generis* Sherman Billingsley, a smooth ex-speak proprietor and former partner of Owney "The Killer" Madden, prohibition vice king, which caters to internationally distinguished literary people, personages high in government, newspapermen, industrialists, stars, financiers, Fair Dealers, labor overlords and millionaire left-wing movie stars, writers, crooners and do-gooders.

There is also the far-famed El Morocco, owned by John Perona, another fabulous ex-speak proprietor, which serves much of the Hollywood and international society glamor set. Rules for admission into its zebra-striped confines are tougher than those for the Union League Club. No man wearing a sport jacket, or sport shirt, or sans tie, has ever been permitted to patronize

El Morocco, regardless of his worldly rank or the size of gratuity pressed on Carino, the dour visaged maître d'. This Cerberus of the door is unimpressed by royalty, nobility, blue blood or Hollywood fame. He bars mobsters and those who look like them; tough guys and babes; noisy ones and pugnacious ones; those overdressed or overplastered. There are no exceptions. When Humphrey Bogart punched a dame who tried to walk off with his toy panda, in El Morocco, he was put on its louse list forever.

But there are clubs in the East Side that get most of their trade from perverts. Models, out-of-work chorines and loafers of both sexes play near by. A few still cater to what is left of the "mob," notably the Copacabana, where Frank Costello throws his lavish parties.

Park Avenue—beautiful, stately and broad boulevard built over the New York Central tracks—has taken up where Riverside Drive left off, as the place to hole up your "keptie."

Oh, yes, there are respectable people on Park—many of them. The per capita wealth of its residents is probably the highest in the world.

If you are an out-of-towner, and you have been slipped a phone number to call by a friend, for a charming companion to keep you company during your stay—at $20, $50 or $100 a night—you will note that the phone exchange is ELdorado, volunteer or REgent, all East Side numbers.

When your guide points out a building as the scene of a particularly gory sex crime, you will invariably find it is on the East Side, probably near the East River.

For Gotham's Tenderloin has moved and changed.

No longer are the rich, lush pickings and pickups around noisy, flamboyant Broadway clubs.

New York has grown up, it seeks its pet pastimes amid surroundings of class, taste and luxury, of which these is plenty in the East Side.

Its shops contain priceless furs and gems, the screwiest and most expensive clothes and hats, the rarest and most unobtainable antiques, furnishings and rugs.

Its well-groomed and deftly made-up and turned-out ladies of leisure come high.

There is more wealth, more splendor, more finery gathered here than in any place on the world in any period of history.

The Sybarites were wrong-side-of-the-trackers by comparison.

A curious phenomenon of the recent war resulted in the greatest collection of treasure in the history of the world being stored in squalid Second and Third Avenue tenement houses, in the upper 40's and 50's, on the East Side.

Soon after Hitler took over, displaced merchants began pouring into America with rare gems, antiques and works of art as their only medium of exchange.

The beginning of war brought a tidal wave of similar fine works to these shores, as British and Continental art dealers moved their stocks here, out of reach of bombers.

New York, already an overcrowded commercial city,

had absolutely no room to accommodate the hundreds of merchants who sprang up to sell these priceless goods. In desperation, they were forced into ground-floor stores of creaky and ratty old buildings in the slum stretches of Second and Third.

But, because this is a strange city, with contrasts in each block, and few well-defined upper class and lower class residential sections, it so happened that right around the corner from these tenements, quite often in the same block, were the apartment homes of the wealthiest folk in the nation—those most interested in buying such wares.

At the time the fabulous goods poured into the country, American millionaires began collecting jewels, art and expensive furniture as a hedge against inflation, on the theory that they always have value and are easily portable.

If you are coming to New York to make a splurge, or learn what life is like, or impress someone on a business deal, you must headquarter on the East Side.

Most any of its hundred standard hotels will do. If you are staying a while, you may want an apartment.

Humorist Harry Hershfield used to explain to his friends that he was "on Broadway, but not of it."

Those were the days when it was considered a rap to say of one "he has gone Broadway."

When one went Broadway (or Hollywood) it wasn't nice at all. He developed a severe case of big-shotitis, spoke of money in tablecloth figures and referred to Lee Shubert as "Lee" and Louis B. Mayer as "Louis" (when they weren't around).

But now, with most of the things that were then so characteristic of Broadway as *de trop* as a pug dog, the people who used to go Broadway go Park Avenue.

It is the same sort of disease, but more aggravated, and when it hits the average guy it raises a higher fever.

You can spot a man who went Park Avenue by the fact that he refers to Alfred G. Vanderbilt as "Alf" and Barbara Hutton as "Babs." He mutters gibberish of "dilatory domiciles" and "married maidens," and has a Social Register.

It has destroyed the usefulness of many otherwise useful people, as will be attested by several East Side night club proprietors.

But one of the queer results of the evolution in fashion is that a lot of society girls from Park Avenue have reverted—and "gone Broadway," becoming models, torch singers and even chorus girls.

The Park Avenue bug usually bites hoi polloi in one of the four or five East Side bistros that cater to the high-tipper set—Stork Club, Colony, Armando's, or El Morocco.

An attaché—say a press agent, headwaiter or even the boss—is swept off his feet by patronage of aristocracy; when the debutantes call him by his first name, the ex-barkeep begins to think of marrying one.

Unless a name is in the Register, he gives it a table in left field. He becomes the complete snob, an insufferable boor, and ends up being a chump to the congenital bluebloods and those who knew him when.

Now, some East Side night spot impresarios are hot to hire D.A.R. names, for tone, réclame and "contacts."

Sherman Billingsley of the Stork once thought it good business to engage a group of society girls to publicize his place.

"Maybe the debs can't do the job as well as the regulars, but they don't go ga-ga when they see a DePuyster," he said. "Besides, even if they don't get printed publicity, their friends come to visit them, which brings in business, which is what I'm in business for."

Not all who "go Park Avenue" are fakes or phonies. For the wealth, the fame and the acclaim that go as rewards for talent, endeavor or outstanding beauty also are on the East Side.

Those who achieve—via business, the arts, or charm —soon find the orbit of life has swung away from Grand Street or 42nd Street, as it had from Sioux City, and now extends from El Morocco to the Stork.

Take the tale of Florence Pritchett, outstanding beauty of two coasts, once reported engaged to young Alfred G. Vanderbilt, before his surprise marriage. Then she went with movie star Bob Walker.

Florence is the product of a small Jersey farm. Back home, like most daughters of plowboys, she dreamed of Broadway, read movie and theatrical magazines, studied the fashions in the slick paper issues.

But she didn't know how to dress or make up.

She came to New York, like many others, in search of big things. But Chance quite often puts gals like her behind a five-and-dime store counter instead of inside a natural mink.

Chance, in the person of John Robert Powers, the models' agent, discovered her. He whipped her into one of the most fashionable young women in town. She quickly became his top number.

She married young Dick Canning, who before the war was associated with an advertising agency which handled the account of the New York Fashion Industry. Dick cleverly arranged a tie-up whereby his lovely wife was provided with the most expensive in the smartest of frocks, coats and hats, which she wore nightly to all the swank clubs. Every day she had a complete, different outfit. Imagine that, girls!—wearing $300 dresses, a new one every day, new $30 shoes, new ermines, new silver foxes, priceless hats.

Florence became the talk of the town. She was welcomed in the most exalted circles. Powers put her in charge of his school, teaching other young girls from farms how to become models. Then Dick Canning went away to war. Florence still had to go out dancing, at the Stork and other gay spots.

After her divorce from Canning, the wealthiest and most eligible young men in New York's swank set began to kneel at Florence's feet.

Florence capitalized on her glamor first as a contact woman for Sam Goldwyn, sent ahead of his super productions to woo publicity, then as a fashion editor, and later as a highly paid radio commentator.

She lost Alf Vanderbilt, but married another Vanderbilt heir, the very rich, very social Earl E. T. Smith.

Though clothes made the gal in Florence's case, Café Society doesn't go in for overdressing. The siren with the extreme hat or costume shrieks like one.

You will find that most best-dressed wrens, aristocrats or successful upstarts, seldom wear hats. While it's socially proper to dress formally, the percentage of those in evening wear in the best spots is definitely below the "fast sets" in rich inland towns.

But what East Siders lack in flash is offset in taste, quality and richness.

A mink coat is the irreducible minimum for a squab who wants to travel in our so-called best circles.

In some spots, ordinary minks have grown so common, it's said the women give them to their maids and take on gray and blue minks. In one club, the gag is that you aren't allowed past the plush rope unless you're wearing a stone marten or platina. Other animals are sent around to the back door.

The East Side's most overdressed crowd was seen at the fabulously successful Monte Carlo, a large portion of whose well-heeled customers were nouveaux riches from New York's golden needle trades market.

This club was born as the House of Morgan, built for the late Helen Morgan by a wealthy admirer. Torchy La Morgan was by then on the way down. The place soon folded and went into bankruptcy. Its premises remained empty until Felix "Fefe" Ferry, Romanian-born producer and promoter, an émigré from Monte Carlo, London and Paris, raised a bank roll to open what was to be the town's most exclusive cabaret.

The new company was underwritten by a score of New York's richest men, on the theory that, as part owners, they would become regular patrons.

A requirement for admission to the bistro was evening clothes.

Now, it is a fact that those who like to dress will not do so under compulsion. Even the stockholders stayed away.

When it went broke, Ferry raised new capital and operated under a less rigorous policy. But the seed had been sown and had taken root.

The real estate firm operating the property decided to take a flyer in the saloon business itself, putting Sam Salvin, son of a successful night club operator of a generation ago, and Dick Flanagan, a happy character with a load of friends, in charge.

The policy was quickly changed. Instead of pitching for the trade of debutantes and scions, notoriously poor spenders, Monte Carlo publicized its herring and wooed the rich dress manufacturers and their ladies. When this fizzled out, another switch was tried—quiet refinement.

Once one of the five top money-making cabarets of the world, it is now shuttered. Its patrons now visit Monte Proser's La Vie En Rose.

William Zeckendorf, president of the firm which owned the defunct Monte Carlo, swung the deal to bring the United Nations to New York over cocktails at one of its corner tables.

Another East Side restaurant patronized by those who know is El Boraccho (The Drunkard), strictly a dining and wining place, fronted and partly owned by Nicky Quattrociocchi, one of New York's odd characters. The money to open the place was put up by

Gracie Fields, the English screen star, and Monte Banks, her husband.

Nicky, a handsome immigrant who barged in 25 years ago from Italy, is a living example of how you can get by in Gotham on wits, nerve and connections.

After a short and desultory career in Hollywood as Theda Bara's leading man in silents, Nicky gravitated to New York, where he was classified a playboy.

He was always neatly dressed, traveled in the correct circles and knew the right people. Yet things were such that once he gave a "Bundles for Nicky" party, to which guests were invited on stationery headed by a list of 1,000 honorary chairmen, and asked to contribute items to help furnish Nicky's 12-room apartment.

Among the suggestions of what Nicky needed were an electric razor, baby grand piano, love seat and cuspidor. The party was a huge success and the apartment couldn't hold all the gifts. One reason was that Nicky's 12 rooms turned out to be a one-room unfurnished flat.

Nicky achieved another kind of renown—more gruesome. He was completely innocent, but a macabre coincidence attended another of his pranks.

Lovely, exotic Helen Kim Mont committed suicide in her Park Avenue apartment. Mrs. Mont had been on the stage under her maiden name, Helen Kim. She was of Korean descent.

As the poisonous fumes were snuffing out the life of this Broadway orchid—bride of 29 days—the lobby of her apartment building was filling up with several hundred gay society folk who had received Nicky's invitations:

"You are most cordially invited to attend a mystery cocktail party which will be given in honor of someone you know, by someone you know. Such a party, with your kind cooperation, should be the most unusual and amusing in New York."

Nicky had sent out the letters, inviting notables to the nonexistent cocktail party, scheduled to start at the hour the beautiful girl chose to end her life in another part of the building.

Stunned by the tragedy, which gave his jest a Grand Guignol denouement, Nicky said:

"I thought it would be a lot of fun to invite them to cool their heels for a while, and then show up. I had no way, of course, of knowing what would happen."

The deadly fumes had just killed Helen when the ermine-wrapped women and their top-hatted escorts began to flock into the building—and the gas emergency crew raced through the lobby.

Nicky started his East Side Restaurant on an investment of less than $5,000. Friends helped him construct the bar. Decorations consisted of labels from whiskey bottles, losing $100 horse race tickets and the lip imprints of women patrons.

The friends he made during his playboy days flocked to the new café, making it an overnight wow. And it never slowed up.

Despite New York's fame for entertainment, but a handful of cabarets catering to New Yorkers present shows, which are considered attractive to only the prairie flowers.

The average East Side café-goer usually doesn't even

want to dance, and when he does he dances only sambas and rumbas, all other steps being passé.

The purpose of dance music in fine clubs is to provide overtones for conversation. For that reason, the bands play pianissimo and all melodies are in one tempo, so you aren't conscious of the breaks.

That's because New Yorkers don't go to clubs for laughs, legs or lilts—they stroll in to dine, drink and talk, to tell their patriots how pretty they are, or even sell a bill to a customer.

When New Yorkers want shows, they go to theatres.

Though we haven't the exact figures at hand, it's a pretty good bet that, per capita, there are more places to purchase liquor around newspaper offices than are to be found in the neighborhood of any other kind of business building.

During the late great drought, the side streets in the East 40's, near Second and Third Avenues, in the vicinity of New York's two largest journals, *News* and *Mirror,* blossomed with speakeasies, so many in fact that one three-story building contained four.

After repeal, a good many of these resorts continued in business as legal saloons, catering mostly to printers, proofreaders and reporters, selling food and drink at moderate prices. Who ever heard of a newspaperman with a spare buck?

Came the war's beef and butter shortage. Ex-speak proprietors with bootleg blood in their veins again heard the stirring call to battle.

Word soon got around that you could always get steaks in these places. Furthermore, there was something bohemian in going to them, because you could rub shoulders with newspapermen and maybe once in awhile see a famed columnist or cartoonist.

Then there were the caricatures on the walls, often drawn by needy members of the craft in payment of booze, and the sawdust on the floor.

New York is a town that follows the leader. Locals began taking their out-of-town friends. Pretty soon you needed reservations and still stood in line, and dingy old saloons boasted doormen, while the journalists who had made the places couldn't wedge in.

The places caught on, and even after the shortages eased the once lowly gin mills continued to draw the carriage trade, considered by everyone in "the know" as the last word in "steakeasies."

Among them are the Palm, Second Avenue and 45th Street, known to initiates as Ganzi's; the Montreal, 45th and Second, known as Colombo's; Pietro's, at 45th and Third, once called The Key Club, because during Prohibition you used your own private key instead of a card; the Pen and Pencil and the Scribes in 45th between Second and Third; and Danny's, the Press Box, and Chris Cella's, between Third and Lexington.

A recent development on the East Side is the looming prominence of Lexington Avenue as a "Main Street." Lexington's rise can be traced in an inverse ratio to Broadway's decline, as the better class of visitor began to select East Side hotels and do his dining and dancing nearby.

Before the war—say a dozen years ago—Broadway

drew a different type of tourist. Then he was a buyer, with fire in his eyes, desire in his blood, and all tabs paid for by the manufacturers and salesmen who were out to give him a better time than did their competitors.

Other visitors were well-heeled Rotarians from the interior and their ladies, here to see the sights and shows and do some shopping.

These people of ample means were Broadway's leaven, keeping it gay and prosperous.

Both large groups dried up during the war. Their places were taken by millions of gaping and gawking servicemen from everywhere, here on leave or passing through, and other millions of defense-plant workers from near-by Jersey, Pennsylvania and Connecticut communities, their pockets bulging with unaccustomed wealth, for the spending of which they had no talent.

It takes many years of practice and some taste and intelligence to make a buck do the things New York can make it do.

These barbarians inundated Broadway. They drove the last remaining residents off the White Way, and with them went much of the flavor of the Stem.

To cater to this horde, which preferred to ankle aimlessly up and down Broadway, eat at hot dog stands and see a movie as the high point of the evening, came shooting galleries, flea circuses, "playlands," photo galleries, souvenir stores with pennants and fancy pillows embroidered with mushy sentiments, grind movies, "sex" bookstores, ham-and-eggeries, portrait artists who paint your picture while you wait, and stands that sell "cocoanut champagne" at a dime the drink.

When the war ended, the "cheap-John" gravy train was over, too. But the better class of visitors never returned to Broadway, which is now forced to get along on a mere dribble of pikers.

The desirables, who began to come back to New York in great numbers, made their headquarters east of Fifth. Lexington Avenue, though one of the narrowest, soon became the East Side's main drag, for many reasons. First, it has more hotels than any other, many of them new, modern and varied in prices. The subway runs under it. Furthermore, both Madison and Park are restricted as to types of window displays and advertising, and electric signs are, as on Fifth Avenue, prohibited.

Third Avenue is still encumbered by the elevated railroad, the only one not torn down to make way for progress, and Second and First Avenues are not only too far east, but are dingy and slummy.

So Lexington is beginning to take on the attributes of a Main Street. It has all-night restaurants and lunch stands, all-night drugstores, and most of the better night clubs are no more than two blocks away, east or west.

Meanwhile, more and more chorus gals and show people, dispossessed by soldiers, sailors and bus-hoppers who have taken over the traditional theatrical hotels near Broadway, are moving to moderate-priced hotels on Lexington, and the Belmont Plaza lobby and drugstore are camping grounds where you can find that blonde, second from the left—the best pick-up spot in New York.

In this eastward move to Lexington is a less glamorous aspect, as the streetwalkers followed in the wake of lonely men. You can see them, afternoon or evening, on the east side of Lexington, from 42nd Street to 57th —swinging big purses and whatever else they have to swing.

Whereas the $5 sisters in sin have inherited Broadway, these are $10-and-upwards snobs.

Another malodorous phase, which now seems the complementary concomitant of a big-town highway, is the horde of homosexuals who adopted it as their midway.

They parade with mincing steps in pairs and trios up both sides of the avenue. Some are blondined, some act "masculine," Negroes mix with white ones, all on the make for strangers.

Gotham's hard-boiled and efficient, but sadly undermanned, police force does its best to keep these misconceived creatures off the streets and out of bars, but there are so many drinking places on the avenue—in some cases ten to a block—it is impossible to make more than token arrests, of the most flagrant cases.

The fame of Third Avenue, a block to the east, is so frequently sung these days in fiction and the movies, that it is not necessary to tell you much about it, except that the so-called sophisticated set has taken over its dingy, old-fashioned saloons under the "El" with the homey Irish names, and driven their former patrons, calloused sons of the pick and hod, far away and muttering.

Here it is considered ultrasmart to drink at a bar where a self-respecting dock-walloper can't afford the new prices.

Here, drinking shoulder to shoulder, are jaded sons and daughters of the rich, bohemians, musical comedy favorites, artists and newspapermen, fairies and Lesbians. There's no room for a plain, honest Irishman.

Things are moving fast on the East Side. Between the time when this tome was started and its last words were written, John D. Rockefeller, Jr., "benefacted" the United Nations into abandoning the original dream of a bucolic world capital to be at home in a series of skyscrapers being designed for the East River front, between 42nd and 48th Streets.

Both authors of this book live within a block of the development. As they work on this paragraph they can see architectural monstrosities being erected on the former site of slaughterhouses, junk-lots and tenements.

Meanwhile, most of its permanent secretariat has taken up living quarters near the world capital-to-be, adding much "atmosphere."

This is a world within a world, with Arabs, Chinese, Haitians, Liberians, Hindus, Siamese—in native dress—mixing in hotel lobbies, restaurants, shops and on the streets, with French, Latin-Americans, Scandinavians, British—and the everyday motley of any New York thoroughfare.

7. WE NEVER GO THERE
ANY MORE

*N*O, *WE* don't. The Bowery, once the storied sinner's paradise, is dead and will not come back. Its glories belong to the past, when New York was young, and, grandpa said, gay.

The wide street under the Third Avenue "El" (soon to be torn down) has been turned over to lofts and salesrooms.

Sandwiched between them are hockshops and the flophouses where homeless hobos rent a clean bed for two bits; and cheap restaurants offer full meals, even in these inflationary days, for the same sum; and filthy bars sell bottled "smoke" at a dime (and an ulcer) a drink.

The only memory of a lurid career of wine, women, song, all-night hubbub and singing waiters (including Irving Berlin) is a lone cabaret: Sammy's Bowery Follies, purposely dressed up in old-fashioned clothes, with lusty, noisy, nostalgic entertainment of the '80's.

In the old days, however, the lines of the song— "The Bowery, the Bowery, they do such things . . ." meant just what they said.

Whereas at one time this zigzag lane had been the center of middle-class night life, with such music halls as Tony Pastor's, and beer gardens, concert saloons and fairly respectable dance halls where the modest toiler and his girl could spend an evening at moderate cost, in its later days the Bowery became the focal point for the worst dives in the city.

Here were low, mean resorts, beside which the dumps of San Francisco's Barbary Coast, New Orleans' Basin Street, and Chicago's 22nd Street were old ladies' homes.

Prostitutes, thieves, dope fiends, and underworlders of every kind made it their headquarters. Murder, suicide, rape, robbery were so common they were ignored by the daily papers, most of which were published a few hundred yards away, on the southerly extension of the Bowery, known as Park Row.

The Bowery gave up the ghost during World War I. Today, even the bums and hobos who are the last of its denizens are getting fewer and fewer, as reflected by the fact that many of the pawnshops are moving or going under.

But when some refined reformers recently started a movement to change the name of the Bowery, so it could shed some of the shadows of its ancient associations, the town rose in indignation against it.

The remaining remnant of the derelicts will not be disturbed. The city coddles them. A Bowery bum is treated with consideration rated by no other bum. The cops carry him from the curb where he has collapsed and lay him tenderly in a dirty hallway; the magistrates are lenient if a pinch is mandatory; the newspapers feature turkey dinners to the old-timers on Thanksgiving and Christmas.

Since even "smoke" has risen in price, the 'bos now buy a pint of domestic wine, 12 per cent alcohol, and mix it with a pint of grain alcohol, and the result is Olympian.

The rubberneck buses are running again, and the spielers sing the sagas of the old cowpath. But they sound hollow. The bum has gone the way of the bison, a vanishing American.

* * *

Dark and dead, like the old Bowery, is Satan's Circus, more generally known as "The Tenderloin."

In less trammeled times, it epitomized wicked all-night life and commercial carnalities too strong even for some gizzards of the period.

Broadway, which then as now, was the show window, bisected it diagonally, but Sixth Avenue was its actual main street.

That long, wide slit (now called The Avenue of the Americas), scheduled by its property owners to be the future rialto, was lined with brothels and saloons from 14th Street to 40th. The lustier aspects of the old Bowery had moved to Sixth Avenue and its environs, and here were hatched the major crimes of the era. The infamous Haymarket dance hall and flesh-market stood at 30th Street.

This section, containing the worst dives in the city and the best theatres, dining places and hotels, was lush picking.

According to the historians it got its name when Police Captain Alexander Williams was put in command of the precinct.

"I been transferred," he is reported to have said. "I

never had nothin' but chuck steak. Now I'm gonna get some tenderloin."

The irresistible upward movement that character-izes New York carried the old Tenderloin above 42nd Street, and for many years there was more gambling, vice and felony in the streets between Fifth and Eighth Avenues, in the 40's and 50's, than in any comparable area in the world.

This came to an end—suddenly—after 1912, follow-ing the notorious Becker-Rosenthal case, when Police Lieutenant Charles Becker was executed in Sing Sing for complicity in the murder of Herman Rosenthal, a big-time gambler who squealed to District Attorney Whitman about the tie-up between police and the crime syndicate.

* * *

Madison Square Garden, where you see the fights, circus and hockey games, is nowhere near Madison Square and is not a garden.

Madison Square is at Fifth Avenue and 23rd Street. The present-day Garden is at 50th and Eighth. A new and larger one is to be built at Columbus Circle.

Long before the huge brick and concrete building you now see was conceived by Tex Rickard, there was the original, memorable Madison Square Garden at 26th Street, on the northeast corner of Madison Square. Its huge arena, like its current relative, housed cham-pionship fights, political conventions and auto shows.

Its chief claim to inclusion in any history of New York lies in the fact that its roof garden contained a

supper club which, to the New Yorkers of the first decade of the 20th century, was a combination of the Stork
and El Morocco of today.

Stanford White, leading artist and architect, had designed it. His glass-ceilinged apartments were in the
building's tower.

One night, 40 years ago, while the popping of champagne corks blended with the soft music of an expensive band, Stanford White was shot to death in the
restaurant.

His killer was Harry Thaw, heir of an immensely
wealthy Pittsburgh family. Thaw, married to Evelyn
Nesbit, most beautiful of the Florodora fillies and immortalized as the Gibson Girl, alleged that White had
seduced his bride before their marriage.

The court battles which followed were classics, and
the story of them is still considered by newspapermen
as the top reporter's assignment of all time.

Evelyn opens and closes, still, at forlorn little cafés.
There are yet traces of her loveliness—only traces.

Thaw died recently. Before his death he lived on a
farm in Virginia and came occasionally to the city he
thrilled, shocked and scandalized. His hair was snow
white. His face was brown as a nut.

8. WHERE MEN WEAR LACE LINGERIE

NOT all who call their flats in Greenwich Village "studios" are queer. Not all New York's queer (or, as they say it, "gay") people live in Greenwich Village.

But most of those who advertise their oddities, the long-haired men, the short-haired women, those not sure exactly what they are, gravitate to the Village.

There are really two Greenwich Villages—the one the sightseer glimpses and the less appetizing one inhabited by psychopaths dimly conscious of reality, whose hopes, dreams and expressions are as tortuous as the crazy curves in the old streets.

"Artistic" sections are a magnet in all cities for tourists and for those who would live *la vie bohème.*

Greenwich Village got an extra shove during Prohibition. The factors which put Harlem on the night-life map also worked out for the Village. It was off the beaten track. Its streets were dark and narrow. Its buildings were old and dingy. A perfect set-up for speakeasies.

The village had once been a ritzy residential section. The Rhinelanders and Wanamakers lived at Washington Square. The Brevoort Hotel was one of the world's most noted. Edward VII, while Prince of Wales, was entertained there in the last century.

Mark Twain lived in a red brick house at Ninth Street.

The city moved northward. Instead of succumbing to the tidal wave of business, the Village became a backwash.

Skyscrapers stayed away. Stables and tumbling shacks remained. But into them came new residents. The district soon became the culture center of New York, and until quite recently, many famed artists, composers, literary lights and show people continued to live there. A few still do.

But a bohemian section always attracts the freaky fringe; those who would live the life of genius without having its admirable attributes, but all its faults and sins.

These, in turn, displaced most of the true intellectuals. In recent years there has been a return to the Village, as modern apartment houses have been run up, especially in lower Fifth Avenue and around Washington Square.

The Village's new "better class" has no more accent on art than on business and politics.

Greenwich Village night life mainly centers around three districts: Sheridan Square, where Fourth Street crosses Seventh Avenue; Eighth Street, between Fifth and Sixth Avenues, and Third Street from Sixth Avenue to West Broadway.

Little bistros and boites, and even a few nationally famed clubs nest at sporadic intervals in almost every byway of the Village.

The best-known resorts of Greenwich Village are no more bohemian than any of the better uptown spots. Jimmy Kelly's, a beaut of a room specializing in fan wielders and dancing gals, is patronized chiefly by merchants and Wall Streeters.

The Village Barn, dubbed the Kathedral of Korn, features entertainment like Omaha and is the favorite haunt of jays from Brooklyn, the Bronx and Weehawken. El Chico is a rumba hangout.

On another plane completely are the joints patronized by the Village variants, where the customers are so mixed up the habitues don't know whether to use the boys' room or the other one.

There are floor shows in which most entertainers are fairies, men playing the female roles.

Many of these are in Third Street, though on Eighth Street, a few feet from the women's prison, is the city's most publicized "queer" joint—the Moroccan Village.

Most female homos' hangouts are in Third Street, and here, in a small, smoky and raucous saloon every Friday night is held a "Lesbian soiree," at which young girls, eager to become converts, meet the initiates.

These parties are presided over by an old and disgusting excuse for a woman, who is responsible for inducing thousands of innocent girls to lead unnatural lives.

It is a law violation for entertainers to appear in "drag" (clothes of the opposite sex). By means of broad burlesque, the regulation is skirted. The swish in wig and dress is okay if the trousers hang down under the gown.

Technically, homos must not gather on licensed premises or be exploited in a floor show.

Until a decade ago, many midtown night clubs presented such shows and catered to the twisted trade. When the cops cracked down, the pouting queens and Lesbians took to Greenwich Village.

There they are not molested by police if they remain in the district and don't bother others, on the theory that you can't do away with them, and as long as they're with us, it's better to segregate them in one section, where an eye can be kept on them. But the most notorious Lesbian night club in New York is on Second Avenue, south of 14th Street, on the lower East Side—the 181 Club.

Here, too, the police are comparatively lax about enforcing the law against female entertainers or hostesses mingling with guests. One reason for this "tolerance" in the Village undoubtedly is due to the fact that there are so many small joints in its narrow streets, it would take a regiment for enforcement.

Another is that in many of the smaller dives it's difficult to tell who is an entertainer and who a customer. All manner of exhibitionists, frustrated hams and undiscovered artists gather in these places. In many, the floor show is almost always impromptu, with most of the entertainment provided free by the guests, especially the "gay" ones.

Between these two levels of honest if Middlesex entertainment are the atmospheric places gotten up to look very Left Bank, with eerie lighting and futuristic painting to impress the pabulum.

"Occasional" prostitutes work some of the bars, and bobby soxers flirt at Washington Square. But most of the pickups in Greenwich Village are those between fags and between skirted women-hunters.

Since the working artistic colony forsook the Village and turned it over to congenital abnormals, the rest of the town seldom, if ever, is invited to Village affairs. All the excitement downtown now is behind closed and locked doors.

Drugs and depravities are prevalent at some of these purple parties, which often turn into unspeakable saturnalias within draped walls, in musk-heavy air.

An uncommonly large percentage of the nation's runaway girls are found in the Village, living with men or women. Recently there has been some Negro penetration. There is no racial discrimination in parts of the section.

In one of the Village's most famed cabarets, Café Society Downtown, the younger boys and girls of both races mingle openly.

This financially successful club had an uptown branch in the swank East Side, where customers also "hopped across the (race) fence." It was shuttered after the president of the corporation owning both clubs turned out to be the wife of America's "No. 2 Communist"—Leon Josephson, convicted of contempt of Congress. The village club is still operated but by new owners—not Red.

But shrewd traders in nature's mishaps profit by the surreptitious reputation of this off-the-highway sector.

They have runners at the clubs and around the town, whispering to likely cash-and-carry strays—women included—of Sodom and Gomorrah on Man-

76

hattan, where, for a stiff price, they can behold forbidden fruit.

When a fish is hooked, a quick 'phone call assembles the male magdalens and the female monstrosities. When the visitor arrives, the revel is in swing, to seem spontaneous. What goes on then is pretty much the real thing. Guests are rarely invited to any indulgence —they are spectators.

Groppe (grape) is served. This is made of the crushed remains of the ingredients of brandy, cheap, insidious and atomic. Whiskey is supposed to be adjured, but this concoction is even stronger, though it doesn't seem so to the tongue and tonsils.

The apartment, often a duplex with couches below and a bed or two on the narrow balcony, is candle-lit. The floor is strewn with exotic rugs. The furniture is individual and often distingué.

Whips, handcuffs, leg-chains, wire brushes and other instruments of sadistic and masochistic physical and moral aberration enter into the play.

It's all routined, timed and stage-managed.

The "privileged" who are "let in" on these practices have paid in advance—lest they are overcome by revulsion and cannot stomach the full show. If they stay through, they are besieged for "luck money," as gratuities are known among these habitues and sons of habitues.

This is the Village—if you care for such.

9. IT'S NOT TRUE

a.—*Chinatown*

THE VISITOR to New York will not find the answer
to the musty gag: "Is it true what they say about Chinese girls?" in Chinatown. The local slant-eyed Sadies
seldom mix with Caucasians; and most of them are so
shy they wouldn't tell you, let alone let you explore
the question.

Almost every other superstition and preconceived
notion you've had about the Chinese and Chinatown is
as counterfeit as chop suey.

Remember the old song about "Chinatown, my
Chinatown, where the lights are low."

Well, they aren't. Chinatown is so brightly lighted,
with gay and multi-hued neon signs, that its few blocks
rival Broadway.

Gotham's Chinatown is the oldest in the world, outside the Orient, and looks it.

Long before there were human habitations where
now is San Francisco, there were suave and placid
Orientals in Gotham.

New York's Chinatown, well over a century old, was
first settled by a small group of Asiatics, stranded on
our shores when a Yankee showman who had brought
them here to exhibit their native customs and handi-
craft, beat it with the boodle.

Venerable tenements, some of which are said to have

been standing when the first Chinese family moved in, more than 100 years ago, line its three crooked, narrow streets.

Though New York houses several times as many Chinese as San Francisco, our Chinatown is considerably smaller and certainly not so lively. Our Orientals are spread throughout the five boroughs of the city in which they work and live, very much like other citizens of this cosmopolitan metropolis. But Chinatown is to them their capital, their county-seat, which most of them visit every Sunday to see friends and relatives, transact business, shop for favorite provisions and stop in at the tong, clan or family clubhouse.

Chinatown boasts many Oriental restaurants, some of world renown, yet it knows no night life. There are more chow mein palaces in the area of Broadway and 50th Street than in Chinatown, and the city's only night club with an all-Oriental floor show, the China Doll, is in West 51st Street.

Chinatown proper consists of three short streets in an irregular triangle: Mott, Pell and Doyer.

Mott Street is in the territory of the On Leong Tong. The Hip Sings, smaller tong, control the other two streets. There are no other tongs in New York, all competitors having been wiped out by the surviving two.

Until 15 years ago, Chinatown was the scene of many gory wars and at times it was dangerous to visit the section. The hatchetmen proved notoriously poor marksmen when they discarded their traditional weapons for automatics. When too many innocents got plugged, the authorities stepped in, and after a threat to deport the whole Chinese colony, a permanent peace was patched up. There have been no wars since, though there is considerable unrest as Communists try to take over the tongs.

The tongs, in their more pugnacious days, might have been compared to the white gangs and mobs that fought each other, with even more ferocious violence, for territorial control of rackets.

Now the tongs are business and social groups, boards of trade or chambers of commerce, as it were. But many members are in dope and gambling.

Today the Chinese are among the most peaceful inhabitants of this polyglot city. Few are arrested for serious crimes, other than narcotic smuggling, in which lawbreakers invariably are sailors from China who speak no English and who are employed by white American criminal syndicates.

New York's Chinese are remarkably well-to-do. The elders of some families are rich even according to American standards, with their money invested in real estate, restaurant and laundry chains.

Chinese on relief are unheard-of, mainly because of a centuries-old custom of family unemployment insurance, whereby those who have jobs help out less fortunate relatives.

Furthermore, Chinese pride and "face" forbid acceptance of gratuities from strangers or public authorities. How backward they are!

Because of respect for family and elders, juvenile

delinquency is practically unknown among New York's Chinese.

The sons of Cathay continue to be "pacifistic" in their dealings with white men. If humanly possible, they avoid contact with the white man's system of courts and police. They settle all their own squabbles according to their own customs and Oriental laws. If both litigants are members of the same social or commercial organization, such as a tong or a family club, the elders arbitrate the argument.

But if they belong to rival organizations, the quarrel is taken to Shavey Lee, so-called "Mayor of Chinatown," or to the Chinese Benevolent Society. If either is unable to work out a satisfactory solution, the Consul General of the Republic of China, with offices in Radio City, is called on to act as a court of final appeal. His verdict is always accepted, though one or both litigants may be American-born, thus American citizens.

Strangely enough, under the provisions of New York State's model arbitration act, most of these decisions by the representative of a foreign government are accepted as law. (Another example of how the Chinese did it first.)

However, should these verdicts be unenforceable in American courts, all Chinese parties observe them religiously. They have to. Failure to do so amounts practically to a death sentence—at least exile. For if a Chinese went contrary to the rules, he would be ostracized from the community and unable to do business with any other member of the community.

If he owned a restaurant, he couldn't hire Chinese waiters, buy Chinese provisions or serve Chinese customers.

There is a movement afoot to tear Chinatown down and relocate its remaining inhabitants throughout the city. The buildings are fire hazards and health menaces. But the Chinese are fighting stubbornly to retain their communal district. They say it is the only Chinatown in America that looks authentically like China. Also, it smells like it.

The visitor who has been to San Francisco's Chinatown first will be struck by the almost complete absence from the streets of our section of Chinese females over the age of 14. New York's Chinatown, much older, is far more conservative than those in other cities, or even in China, where the world has moved.

Our Chinese women spend most of their time in the home (which is regrettable, because they are dainty and pretty) while their men are out in the world.

There is far less intercourse between Chinese and whites here, also for that reason. Chinese parents try to keep their daughters away from white men, though in San Francisco, because Chinatown is so intimately connected with the life of the city, it is a commonplace to see them out together.

Naturally, taboos are breaking down as high school and college girls demand the right to associate with their schoolmates, regardless of race.

The tallest and most beautiful girl in Chinatown is Louise Leung, a model and showgirl.

Chinese are inveterate gamblers for high stakes.

Some of the biggest craps, poker, gin rummy, fan tan and mahjong games in New York are played in Chinatown. But only between Chinese.

The cops are tolerant if no whites cut in. Many shops are merely fronts for gambling in the rear. The store shelves are almost completely bare of merchandise and if you should have the temerity to wander in and try to buy one of the few items kept as dressing, you'd annoy the proprietor greatly. That is, if you could get him out front, away from his game.

Just to keep the record straight, occasional arrests are made, but after the players pay their dollar fines they go right back to their cards.

In so far as the white population of New York is concerned, there is absolutely no Chinese prostitution in Chinatown. Yet many flats in the narrow streets are maintained with girls smuggled from the Orient as picture brides, expressly for entertainment of the local Chinese males.

The authorities know all about it, but look the other way so long as none but Chinese patronize the houses.

The local male Chinese far outnumber the females, and such places are considered a necessity.

A new traffic has come to the region. "Come to" is what's new about it.

The cops and courtroom loungers have long called prostitutes "flesh-peddlers." This appellation was never quite true. Inmates of houses, when there were such things, "sat for company"—the men came to them. Women who pounded the flagstones were peddlers only to a degree, as they had to be surreptitious, attract with a smile or glance, then be "solicited" to some extent.

But now, in Chinatown, young Puerto Rican girls are sent to bring themselves and offer themselves, to display their merchandise on the spot and to haggle over the price.

They go from house to house, floor to floor, door to door. They knock. If a woman answers (there are few instances of that) they say, "Sorry, mistake." If a man opens the door, the caller asks, "Want nice girl here?"

Some of these peddlers are in their early 'teens, for Caribbean females blossom young.

They are sent forth by their lovers, by their husbands, some by their own parents, to garner the dough.

In Little Spain sex is cheap, selling it is precarious and competition is not only voluminous, but perilous, for the girls will fight with knives over a prospect.

So the Puerto Ricans went hunting for a market and found it among the Chinese, underwomaned thirty or forty to one, racially conspicuous, so they cannot go forth into the byways, let alone the highways, on the hunt.

The secret of the new system, self-delivered sex, wasn't long kept dark.

The downtown hoodlums began to lie in wait for the girls after they had made their rounds, to beat them up and take their money from them. So now the girls, after one Mission Mott Street, book themselves ahead, dating each flat for the next duty tour—and they have the Chinese buy postal money orders, made out to them, individually, against the next visit. These are not cashable except by the beneficiary without running into trouble with the Feds, and the toughest canaille shudder away from that.

So the flesh-peddlers' profits now get to Little Spain.

The hick who takes in Chinatown from a sightseeing bus is led first to the Rescue Society for Bowery bums, which, according to the guide, is located in what was once an opium den.

Then he is shown a joss house, in back of the China-town post office, and he is told about the maze of secret tunnels which are supposed to connect most of the buildings in the area, for use during tong wars, opium or Prohibition raids.

The modern generation of American-born Chinese never smelled, let alone smoked, opium, and few of the old-timers remain. Occasionally you can spot one, a bent, wizened, broken and prematurely old fellow who stands out like a barn alongside his non-indulging brethren, who have the Chinese gift of seldom showing their age.

Concubinage is permitted under Chinese law, and some of the older, wealthier Chinese own an extra wife or two, or even a slave-girl brought over from the old country. But these are things you can't prove, and any-way, it's done uptown by the white folk, but under a different name.

Even in these days of sulfas and vitamins, most Chi-nese still believe in herb therapy. Maybe they're not so wrong. Many important drugs in the modern pharma-copoeia were discovered in Cathay, centuries ago—ephedrine is but one.

Chinatown herb dealers also sell concoctions guaranteed as love potions, aphrodisiacs and virility nostrums. Perhaps there's something to their formulae. The population of China is 450,000,000.

New Yorkers eat more Chinese food per capita than any other occidentals; more Chinese food is sold here than that of any other foreign origin.

Favorite is chow mein, with chop suey a poor second. Neither of these glutinous creations is indigenous. Both are American inventions. The Chinese themselves, and those who know good food, never eat either mongrel dish. You are spotted as a neophyte if you order them.

The authentic Chinese menu contains hundreds of exotic items, made of everything from eels to birds'-nests. If you want to play safe and not show your ignorance call for *mo gu gai pan,* which is a distant cousin to chicken fricassee.

Though Chinese men drink considerable potent spirits, women of the race seldom, if ever, imbibe. They say it makes their faces red—and it does. Their men discourage them from drinking, but white wolves, aware of the effect of champagne on slant-eyed dolls, try to load them with it, often with encouraging results.

The Chinese call us "white devils," *lo fan* or *fan guey,* and their word for wolf is *chai long.* Their favorite drinks are *mui kai low* and *ng ga pai.* Don't try either unless you possess a strong stomach.

b.—*Little Tokyo*

Before the war, there were few Japanese in New

York. Most of them were treaty merchants, technicians or students, who evaporated with Pearl Harbor.

But then came the influx of Japs from the West Coast states. As many as 10,000 are reported to have moved here after being released from relocation centers, while countless thousands more came East before the final deadline to vacate Pacific areas. There was no Jap-baiting here. Many have since gone home.

There had been no "Little Tokyo" here. Now there are at least three small ones in Manhattan, alone.

The most concentrated one is in 65th Street, near Broadway, in the heart of the Filipino colony. Another, but sporadic, Jap settlement runs from 18th to 23rd Streets, near Ninth Avenue. A third group lives on the upper West Side, from Columbia University southward into the 90's and 80's where there are several Japanese churches, Christian, Shinto and Buddhist, and northward into Washington Heights.

Since the war, the Japs have taken an even less active place in the community than do the Chinese. Few are merchants or storekeepers. They, however, mix more freely with whites. The girls, especially, are found working in American offices, hospitals, hotels and even in show business, where many of the "Chinese" acts really are Japanese.

There are three Nipponese restaurants in New York, specializing in such concoctions as *suki yaki,* the national dish, and *saki,* the national knockout. These operated unhindered all during the war and were patronized by Americans and Chinese as well as Japs.

Miyako's in 56th Street, just west of Fifth Avenue, is internationally famous.

Among New York Japs there is considerably less resentment against the relocation than appears on the West Coast. Those resident here before the war and those who came shortly after Pearl Harbor escaped confinement in concentration camps completely, while those who were shut in for short periods missed the worst of the indignity.

In this tolerant city, even during the height of the war, they found sympathy and encouragement and employment. With few exceptions, white neighbors treated them hospitably. They were not made to feel like a special, inferior class.

Even the Chinese welcomed them and gave them employment.

For that reason, the young Nisei in New York is less apt to be a sucker for Communist propaganda than his more bitter cousin on the West Coast. There are, it is true, a few leftish Jap youth groups here, suspected of being under Red domination, but most of the local Nisei disavow the movement, and resent attempts of radicals to involve them in an all-out anti-white movement, together with other dark peoples.

As noted, Japanese maidens are considerably less shy than their Chinese sisters, and more frequently mix with white men. Many local connoisseurs of Oriental beauty prefer Japanese women to Chinese, for, though it is practically impossible to detect a physical difference between them, the Jap girls are said to be more feminine, fun-loving and lively. Some of the outstanding "Chinese" girls at the defunct China Doll café were Japanese—notably Ann Koga, Katherine Kim, Trudy Kim and Tobe Kai.

c.—*Koreans*

Your authors once read somewhere that Korean women are supposed to be the most beautiful in the world. The expert who so stated said, "Ask any sailor, if you don't believe me." Since then scores of service men have written us to say it ain't true.

The New York Korean colony is small. Though there is a Korean church near Columbia University, there are said to be no more than 100 permanent residents of that race in the city. The number is slightly swelled by a few students, most of whom reside at International House, and frequent visitors from Honolulu.

Many work in Chinese restaurants. Some of the prettiest "Chinese" girls in show business are Koreans. At least one, June Kim, was a Ziegfeld Follies girl. Lovely Florence Ahn is a noted singer.

d.—*Corregidor*

The Filipino colony extends from 63rd to 72nd Street, approaching on Broadway. There are few Filipino women in New York, and for that reason the district is known to abound in disorderly houses.

Though many of their own women are as dainty as Japanese dolls, which they greatly resemble, most Filipino men seem to prefer blondes, big billowy-bosomed, over-painted ones. Many in that category are supported on a group or communal arrangement, each by several Filipino boys.

Well, some white gents keep several babes!

It's a difference in customs. Economics probably is at the bottom of it.

And half a blonde is better than none.

10. AROUND THE WORLD
IN NEW YORK

AS *BEFITS* the most cosmopolitan city on earth, you can dine, wine, dance, make love, gamble or raise hell or children in practically any language you choose in New York.

In the one block of West 49th Street, between Sixth and Seventh Avenues, you will find bistros serving these native foods: Singhalese, Chinese, Jewish, French, Spanish, Mexican, Italian.

But the blood from the pulsating heart of New York's 8,000,000 doesn't pump only into the main arteries.

There are some 1,500 licensed cabarets in the city and some 20,000 saloons. These are scattered over all five boroughs. In many localities, especially those inhabited by foreign racial groups, miniature Broadways have sprung up, reminiscent of main drags in foreign countries.

a.—*Beer und Pretzels*

Clustered around Third Avenue and 86th Street in the heart of Yorkville, is the German section. Here there are dozens of beer halls, with waiters in native costume and fat, funny Brünnhilde sopranos singing Viennese waltzes and Bavarian seidel-songs.

Before Hitler, Yorkville was a fad. Prohibition was only an English word, untranslatable. The "Hoboken

91

steam beer" was potent, spiked with ether before your eyes by the waiter with an eye-dropper. One visitor asked, "Hey—where's the operation that goes with this?"

We used to call the people we saw there "gemüt-lich," which means homey, and talk about their quaint costumes and customs and placid way of life.

Later—when lists of Nazis were released—we saw many of these stolid heinies on record. Though outwardly all Yankee light and love, the district is still a hotbed of Nazi fanaticism, though you hear few talk about it, even after a dozen beers.

The younger generation, of course, is solidly American and resentful of the old folks' European ways.

Other but smaller German sections abound throughout the city, notably in the Bronx and in Queens. In the latter borough were some of the most rabid pro-Nazis in the country. Here some of the German spies who landed from a submarine during the war were sheltered.

Many Lutheran churches in the Bronx and Queens conduct all their religious services in the German tongue.

A smaller and older German colony survives on the Manhattan East Side, between 14th and 23rd Streets. These are no newcomers; some of their restaurants trace back to the days when liberty-loving Germans escaped from Prussian feudalism in 1848.

One of the most famous eating places in the world and one of the oldest in New York is Luchow's, at 14th Street and Irving Place. Here, in several spacious rooms, occupying a block, is a memory of gracious, graceful days now unfortunately gone forever.

Eating is an art at Luchow's, undisturbed by raucous talk or jive. Instead, there is the pleasing music of a three-piece stringed aggregation which plays waltzes and operas and drinking songs. Luchow's features 14 different kinds of beer on draught and was the first American restaurant to obtain genuine Rhine wine and Pilsener after the war.

Throughout the years its guests have been the New York great, leaders of art, literature, finance and politics. George Jean Nathan and Henry Mencken eat there once a week, a practice they began almost a half century ago with Huneker, the great critic.

The menu is heavy with rich German dishes; the decor is strictly Teutonic. But the present owner of Luchow's is a Swede from Washington.

b.—*Borscht and Blintzes*

Second Avenue, south from 14th Street, is the Main Stem of the Russian, Romanian and Jewish lower East Side. A score of night clubs are here, many of national repute, presenting floor shows comparing favorably with the biggest.

The eating places are patronized by connoisseurs from everywhere, who relish European dishes.

There are theatres in Second Avenue presenting drama, musicals, revues and vaudeville, in Yiddish, where world-famed artists appear.

Second Avenue is as brightly lighted with neons as

Broadway, and its shops display wares as costly as those on Fifth Avenue.

The people who patronize this gay way are imbued with the traditions of the old lands. Here, there is little whiskey drinking; wines and beer are preferred, along with a leisurely dinner, and pinochle afterward.

Vice does not thrive here, because the young blades seek it elsewhere. They find their legitimate amusement uptown, too, leaving the lower East Side almost entirely to the old folks, who are too set in their ways to want or appreciate the hurried pleasures of the Americans.

As these lines are being typed, at the corner of Henry and Pike Streets, in the very core of what once was the most famous American ghetto, lies the collapsed remains of a five-story synagogue.

It just gave up, after a hundred years of service, and tumbled into rubble.

The amazingly significant feature of this incident is that, though it happened on a Saturday afternoon, nobody was injured. The building, though still actively functioning, was empty.

This, on the Jewish day of rest and worship, gives you an idea of how time has changed the ways of that section of Manhattan into which poured the millions fleeing the pogroms, the Cossacks and the other European elements of outrage which made New York the largest Jewish population center in the world.

From the numbered streets beginning with First, down to the old commercial district, and from the

Bowery to the East River, about 600,000 Jews, nine-
tenths of them European refugees, lived for generations
in squalor, dirt and congestion. Most of them followed
devoutly their orthodox faith and rituals. No razor
ever touched a male face. Girls from the marriageable
age onward never exposed their hair, but hid it under
wigs. All activities ceased Friday at sundown, after
which, until dark on Saturday, no Jew could carry anything in his pockets—money, watch, keys, even a hand-
kerchief. No Jew could light a fire or a candle or a
lamp. For heat and illumination, Gentiles were hired
and paid to strike the matches.

On Sunday, when the rest of the town was still, the
ghetto bristled with business, trade, the myriad sweat-
shop operations—which were largely carried out in the
rooms in which families slept, ate and lived—and the
Jewish population was a community set apart, neither
adopting the manners of others nor proselytizing them
to assume theirs.

Fifty synagogues flourished, some of them handsome
and imposing, though the Jews in the main were mis-
erably poor. Intermarriage with other races was un-
heard of. The Jews had their own banks and stores and
mechanics, who kept their calendar and who spoke
their language, Yiddish, which has a universal base,
though it wanders off into a dozen different dialects,
mainly of European derivation.

Today, all that has changed so that there are scarcely
a fifth of those of Hebrew descent in the area and virtually the only ones who practice any of the habits of
their forefathers are a handful of refugees who man-

aged to get here since Adolf Hitler began to persecute so-called "non-Aryans" under the drive of his mad megalomania.

For decades, as the Jews became more prosperous, they scattered to better homes in upper Manhattan, the Bronx and Flatbush, where they penetrated into every walk of American life and became active in commerce, politics, arts and letters, journalism and even pugilism. About one-third of the old territory into which they originally huddled for mutual comradeship and protection has been razed for modern ideal apartment developments. Another substantial segment has disappeared under the advance of commercial construction. And what is left is largely the habitat of big business, which includes some manufacturing but is devoted mostly to jobbing and retailing, some of it on a tremendous scale.

Jewelry and furs are sold in magnificent stores, especially on Grand Street. The merchandise is frequently advertised in the regular daily press and among the customers are the dowagers and debutantes from the smartest sectors of the city.

The remainder of those who still choose to live in this teeming, malodorous and entirely alien stockade without walls constitutes a unique contingent in New York and American life.

That this was once the center of aristocracy during the pre-Revolutionary British occupation is attested by the names of the streets which still appear on the corner signs: Pitt, Eldridge, Norfolk, Suffolk, Stanton, Essex, Broome, Rivington, Delancey, Rutgers and Elizabeth. But one has been added—Houston Street—which is pronounced Howston, though named after Sam Houston, and the downtowners will never change it.

On the once mansioned Pitt Street and for eight square blocks is New York's gypsy colony—thieving, bootlegging tricksters who do no useful work, who are unbelievably soiled and live 15 and 16 in a room, a vacant store or a cellar. Conditions here are far worse than in Harlem because most of these are illiterates and by some strange ruling, their children are not sent to American schools.

They have picturesque ceremonies for weddings, births and funerals, though all of these are common and frequent enough. For important funerals the tribes gravitate here from all parts of the country. Rejoicing, lamentation and just plain drunken disturbances are of no concern to the police. The gypsies pay no taxes and do not even vote. But they seem to enjoy a feudal duchy almost as immune against authority as it is against soap.

Surrounding them are specialized little Jewish groups, mostly arrivals within the last dozen years, comprising Jews of Galician, Russian, Romanian, Hungarian, Polish, Latvian, Lithuanian and Ukrainian origin. These are excellent, thrifty, industrious people who bridge the chasm of foreign tongue and customs by hard work, a stubborn pride in their old-country ways and staunch worship of their God and the teachings of their church.

They occupy the only islands in this historical portion of New York with local rabbis whom they maintain from their meagre earnings, mostly at new trades which they had to acquire in this mechanized civilization after they had fled from the primitive villages and fenced-in cattle-corrals of the larger European centers.

Unlike many of the Americanized, American-born young GI's who cheerfully joined the 52-20 contingent, these oldsters do not go on relief. They appreciate the blessings of freedom and sincerely try to pay for them by good and upright citizenship even before they can become citizens.

All around them they see grocery, delicatessen and butcher stores run by their co-religionists, with ham and bacon in the windows.

They mutter in their beards over the moral decadence of the youth. They are teased and taunted by the young Jews as cruelly as, generations ago, all Jews were mistreated by their Gentile neighbors, especially the Irish during the heavy immigrations that followed the potato famines and divided this whole section into an unending battlefield. The Jews by tradition are not cowards, though they have through modern history been compelled to be on the defensive as a minority everywhere.

Out of these early conflicts rose some of the toughest and most murderous gangsters in American history—Little Augie, Kid Dropper, and the Murder, Inc. mob led by Lepke and Gurrah. Once they learned they had to battle, they became fierce warriors with knife, gun and every other equipment.

There are still four Yiddish daily newspapers, all prosperous and all with different policies as to politics, orthodoxy and the never-ending controversy of the Jew in every land to which he drifts—assimilation.

One organ pleads for organization and Americanization, even intermarriage and decentralization of the ghetto; another is passionately for rigid maintenance of Jewish customs and traditions and all the age-old tenets, such as Sabbath observation, kosher food, even the *mikveh*, according to which every married and marriageable female is expected to bathe in a community establishment at certain times.

Between the completely "emancipated" and the extremely orthodox there still remains a segment which has cut away from the old but still fears to ignore completely the God of Israel.

As a result there are thousands of Jews who pay no heed to the ways of their forefathers excepting on the high religious holidays—Yom Kippur, Rosh Hashana and the Passover. For these there is a rush to get room in the few remaining synagogues. It is not impossible that the ticket scalpers will yet take these bonanza days over.

One of the pet stories having to do with this condition is told of a shabby little tailor who rushed up to the "schul," the synagogue, on one of these holy days. The pews had been sold weeks in advance at high rentals. The sexton stepped in and barked: "Ticket!" "I have no ticket." "If you have no ticket you can't get in." "But I got to get in. I got to see my rich brother. He is in there." "That's a lot of hooey." "But I tell you I got to see my brother—it's a matter from life and death." "Well, if it's life and death O.K. Go in and see

99

your brother and come right out . . . and don't you let me catch you praying!"

c.—*The Not-So-Blue Danube*

Upper Broadway, from 72nd Street to 110th, is now a mid-Europe in miniature. Many of those who sought refuge here during the 1930's—especially Austrians, Czechs and Hungarians—settled thereabouts and the atmospheric night life of middle Europe followed.

Here are stores that sell the delicacies of Central Europe and pastry shops where fat, but stylishly turned-out women gorge on rich chocolate sweetmeats washed down by the white wines of Tokay, the Rhine and Moselle.

This part of town was once one of New York's finest. Riverside Drive is one of the grand avenues of the world, with a view across the broad Hudson toward the palisades of New Jersey.

The castle of Charles M. Schwab has been demolished. The fine tree-lined West End Avenue, and upper Broadway with its grassy center lane, all are frayed and frowzy.

Now a score of small and medium-sized clubs purvey what purports to be the food and entertainment of Vienna, Budapest, Bucharest, Prague and Sofia.

But it mostly boils down to a gypsy fiddle and a bowl of goulash.

d.—*Little Italy*

Not long ago, the center of Italian life was Mulberry

Street, near the historic Five Points and police head-quarters. Here one went in search of such Italian deli-cacies as pizza and ravioli.

In the years between the two World Wars, older im-migrants gradually became Americanized. Italians, last of the large racial groups before the Puerto Ricans came to colonize, soon became one of the most popu-lous and most dominant minorities.

Little Italys took root all over the five boroughs. Italian restaurants blossomed forth in every part of town, to run the Chinese chop suey parlors a close race for the trade of those who like exotic foods.

The sons and daughters of Italy went into show busi-ness, trade and politics, and their domination extended to vice, crime and gangsterism, but also to the sciences and fine arts.

It is scarcely an exaggeration today to speak of all New York as one huge "Little Italy."

But the old world colony is still centered around Mulberry Street, running north from Canal and west from the Bowery. Here is the acrid odor of Naples—garlic and garbage, dirty restaurants, plump, dark-eyed hookers, evil billiard halls and saloons where a pint of red ink still sells for two bits and you don't have to park your stiletto at the door.

Another fragrant little Italy skirts the borders of Greenwich Village.

But in ex-Congressman Marcantonio's East Harlem the poorest and most crime-ridden Little Italy in all the world begrimes New York.

e.—*Stromberry Poy*

Though Greece was a land of noble statesmen and warriors, most of her sons who settled in New York are engaged in the less exalted though more necessary work of filling hungry American bellies.

A large proportion of the fruit and vegetable business, wholesale and retail, is controlled by Greeks; lunch rooms and cheaper restaurants are almost Greek monopolies.

However, oddly enough, many Hellenes make their living in the huge needle-trades industry. A majority of fur workers are Greek, though most of the plants are owned by Jews.

There are self-made Greek millionaires, too; but they live on estates in Westchester when they are not on their ranches in California.

The hub of the Greek colony is in 58th Street, from Eighth to Ninth Avenues, with restaurants, hotels and bawdy houses. No place for any but Hellenes. English spoken, but seldom understood. Another Greek settlement is at 42nd Street and Eighth Avenue, near the fur market.

f.—*Modern Babel*

The map of midtown Manhattan is more of a racial hodgepodge than the Balkans ever were, with cabarets, eating places (see Appendix F) and wenches in every idiom.

One of the city's largest French sections is in the 40's, west of Eighth Avenue, with little ground floor bistros in musty old rooming houses and broads smelling of powerful perfume.

Armenians and Turks, historic enemies, live and eat in the 20's, on the East Side, near Lexington, and the Hungarian section is in the east 60's before you come to Yorkville. Here the females are fat.

The corner of 110th and Fifth, with its West Indian population, looks like the seamy side of any large Caribbean town, and stinks worse.

There are Persians living in East 58th Street.

International House, near Columbia University, at Riverside Drive and 122nd Street, houses students and visitors from all sections of the globe and of all colors, shades and varieties.

Men live in one wing, women in the other, and if the steel door which separates them, but is never locked because of fire regulations, is opened, a bell clangs throughout the building. (Hell of a Good Neighbor policy!)

11. BLACK GHETTO

THERE were Negro freemen on Manhattan Island before the Revolutionary War. New York never was a station in the abolitionist underground.

The race was represented by only a few scattered thousands at the beginning of the present century. The heavy influx began shortly thereafter in a drive by industry seeking cheap labor.

Agents were sent to the South to recruit whole trainloads of black people to throw into unskilled work against the Irish, Italians and others who were already becoming troublesome to the industrial moguls with demands for higher wages. The pay spurned as too low by the whites looked big to the cotton pickers and ditch diggers of Dixie.

The Negro population grew rapidly. So did the spirit of resentment and hatred which surrounded them everywhere, despite the Northern fiction of race equality.

Not only were the Negroes driven together for protection against a powerful prejudice which kept their lives miserable and unsafe, but they found themselves caught in a ring, welded by small and big owners of real estate, which literally caged them in.

The net result has been the most congested ghetto on the American continent—Harlem.

In the tiny area of Harlem there is now a population of around 650,000—approximately that of the full census of Pittsburgh or San Francisco proper.

There has been practically no new housing built there in decades. The crumbling firetraps, almost all of them still owned by whites, and many by millionaires, have seen little improvement in provisions for sanitation, much less for human comfort. But per room, the rents exacted often equal many in the luxury edifices of gilded Park Avenue.

These thousands of dark-skinned people are truly displaced persons—held in a concentration camp surrounded by the barbed-wire fence of ironclad prejudice. But they attend free schools. They go to the polls. Therefore, maneuvered by slick politicians, white and black, they have become an enormous power. But little of this power is used for their benefit.

Until some 20 years ago tradition and the memory of Abe Lincoln made almost every Negro anywhere a Republican. The Republican machine in New York took this for granted and counted in the Harlem votes automatically before the elections.

A metamorphosis began with the organization of the American Labor party and the growth of the Communist party. These radical groups were weak and poor. They had no hope of electing anyone, and therefore could promise anything to everyone. Negroes, who had nothing to lose, began to be attracted.

For the first time they found themselves wanted, courted, flattered.

The Republicans suddenly woke up to find Harlem slipping away. They joined the parade, and held out new big promises of patronage. They suddenly grew conscious of social obligations, too, a new line for the G.O.P.

Everyone hopped the bandwagon in this new crusade—for the Negro vote. But the Negroes had been inflamed over their grievances and preferred to nurse them, now that self-seekers had acknowledged and emphasized them. Besides, the Republican party never won local elections anyway.

On the crest of this wave rose a shrewd little opportunist named Fiorello H. LaGuardia. He took over Harlem as a private preserve with a fusion of both the Republican and A.L.P. bodies of New York. After he was elected mayor, he sent to Congress, to succeed him from the fringe of Harlem, one Vito Marcantonio, a stooge who had worked in his law office.

With Marcantonio the local leader (State Chairman of the A.L.P.) and LaGuardia for a round dozen years in the City Hall, the pay-off began. The unfortunate Negroes, who had been cuffed and confined so long, were suddenly silk-gloved and pampered, made virtually immune from the police and the law. In this tight little empire ruled by the LaGuardia-Marcantonio axis, everything went, short of, and sometimes including, murder in the first degree.

Harlem, which had once been notoriously frustrated, now sprang into a peculiarly privileged status in reference to the city's laws.

Those of the dark-skinned citizens who were eager to lead decent and normal lives for themselves and their children found the situation worse than before.

Instead of emancipation from the sordid conditions in which they were confined, the political need to keep them in one district was added to their bonds. And they saw their disreputable elements abetted in lawlessness.

Here were some 260,000 votes in one bag. The political sharks knew just the way to play to make them stay put.

The results were disastrous, as many dismayed respectable Negroes found, especially among the growing youth. The police, who carried night sticks in the lobby of Madison Square Garden and Grand Central Palace, pounded the flagstones of Harlem empty-handed and all but handcuffed.

The meekness and silent suffering which had marked the Negroes in a city of a hostile majority went with the new wind. They got practically nothing tangible from their new protectors. The bad physical conditions remained, the conspiracy of prejudice which imprisoned them remained. But their emotional release and mounting anger against their wrongs grew. That crime and immorality under these bizarre conditions should increase was inevitable.

This metamorphosis was taking place during the later years of Prohibition, when lawlessness was smart, sin a laugh, and decency a joke. In their landlocked area of poverty and congestion, when gangsters, flappers and gigolos were symbolic and many college boys were getting out of hand throughout the country, young Harlem threw away the book.

Decent Negroes, seeking only a normal existence,

were appalled. But the tough elements had the support of the dominant political power; and Harlem was a trap from which few could escape.

An occasional Negro was appointed to public office; a few got into civil service; a dribble made the professions. But by and large the wretched economic and social conditions of the race remained, and remain today, not greatly changed over the plight of the race a generation ago.

Today, Harlem is a politician's stronghold. The ward heelers, their bosses and their friends rate high political favoritism. Harlem has this kind of equality, but no other.

The result has been sad.

As this chapter proceeds, the authors will not attempt to review in connection with each incident or observation the abnormal and unique circumstances which have corrupted much of the life of this gigantic Negro concentration camp. They will proceed to tell of Harlem as they know it and have seen it. In Harlem, of course, are many thousands of God-fearing Negro families thoroughly dismayed by the violence, vice and excesses which now exist there, and which will probably continue to exist as long as Harlem remains the exploited landlocked island that it is. Many who could took their families to the Sugar Hill district, where live the more prosperous Negroes, or to the several tree-shaded streets where life continues to flow by rather quietly and respectably.

But in other sections of the district, robbery, rape and murder are rampant and raw. Prostitution is scan-

dalous. With certain elements, assault has become not
only a profession, but a pastime.

The New York newspapers, by common habit, rarely
publish anything about Harlem crime. The city editor
looks at the address and spikes the item.

Police shrug their shoulders and turn their backs
not only on complaints, but on misdemeanors and
felonies within their own sight. This is especially true
where no whites are involved.

Shortly after the outbreak of the war, Harlem was
made out of bounds for white service personnel, with
armed M.P.'s and S.P.'s stationed at close intervals.
Night life became practically one hundred per cent
Harlem-patronized.

The days when a metropolitan black belt was picturesque and novel are gone. The decade and more
when low-class and high-priced slumming in black-
and-tan dives was a big-city fad has passed, too.

Today, Harlem's chief attraction is the famous
Savoy Ballroom. This is not a taxi dance hall. There
are no hostesses or hired partners. The gents bring
their own dames or pick up unaccompanied girls, who
also pay their way in. Most of these are not out-and-
out hustlers. In the old days the Savoy was a wow. The
unrestrained dancing and the first roots of jive and
boogie-woogie were beginning to appear. Both the
music and the hoofing were fascinating to outsiders.
But now few whites come to the doors of the Savoy, and
those who do are firmly discouraged from entering.

America stole the Negroes to work the land it stole
from the Indians. It has not played white with either.

The living, throbbing Harlem—110th Street, 116th Street, 125th Street, 135th Street, Seventh Avenue, Lenox Avenue, the west side of Fifth Avenue from 110th Street up—those highways which in their time have known throngs of sightseers, which in the heyday of Harlem hotspots housed cabarets and after-hour joints known around the world, are now beset by gangsters, streetwalkers, sluggers and muggers who often bash and slash for the mere mischief and sadism of inflamed imagination and unbridled, coddled encouragement to misbehave.

On these and the dimly lit side streets which cross them property and life are rarely safe.

Here white detectives dare not travel except in pairs; here rent-collectors dare not go about or enter buildings without cops to guard them; here is no place for sightseers or any strangers.

Here rove the numerous gangs, members ranging in number from a dozen to several hundred and in age from almost babyhood to the "heavy workers," who include many ex-convicts.

Harlem first got on the map as a place to have fun during the 1920's, when an imaginative fellow named Lee Posner, who later adopted as a middle name "Harlemania," saw its possibilities after the Chicago "black-and-tan" fad had risen to popularity. Jack Johnson, the ex-heavyweight champion, had a saloon on Seventh Avenue. This became the Cotton Club which, with all Harlem, started toward worldwide fame.

Prohibition was in effect if not in force, but the snoopers passed this district up.

The black part of Harlem was tucked away in the northern half of what is now the section. Its main cross street, 125th, was still lined with fine shops and branches of downtown department stores. Below that thoroughfare old New York families still lived and there were excellent apartment buildings and elegant residences.

By 1930, the Negroes had everything from 110th Street up to the Polo Grounds, at 155th Street, to themselves.

Repeal brought a change to Harlem's night life. The fad had worn thin and the attractions of unlimited liquor and no set hours had faded. Some of the glitter spots moved downtown—Connie's Inn, the Cotton Club, the Ubangi. New cabarets with all-Negro talent began to spring up in the center of town.

When the casual pleasure-seekers forsook Harlem, a few wise boys took over in side-street locations. New York's legal liquor and cabaret closing deadline has been 4 A.M., since repeal. But that was too early for some, especially those connected with the major night clubs, who quit work at that hour and then wanted to play.

Harlem, which was not being called to account on police regulations, took up where the big ones left off.

Many of the remaining joints didn't put on their first shows until after 4 A.M., and they remained open as late as the last customer could lift a glass. Your authors remember often leaving such places at 10 or 11 o'clock next morning, climbing out of a smoke-filled and dingy basement into broad daylight, their eyes smarting.

It was in this period that the "ofays," Harlem's word for whites, began mixing openly. Several female name stars were soon notorious for such habits.

There are very few houses of commercial prostitution in Harlem. They are not needed. Women are too easy to pick up. And they don't have to be picked up.

A man of the world can spot a whore by instinct, no matter what her color. But the Harlem wenches refuse to credit so much intelligence. They have a hundred brazen approaches. One of the commonest is to lead a little dog on a leash, and as a white man comes within hearing, ostensibly addressing the dog, she says:

"You come on with me now. You come on right in the house with me."

If there is any doubt as to what or whom she means, she is dangling the key to her apartment in her other hand. From this up to the most ancient methods, straightforward or from the corner of the mouth, "How'd you like to have a good time, mister?" they fear neither daylight, nightlight nor darkness.

This of itself shocks no one, least of all those whose names are on the cover of this book.

But back of it is a great deal more than the danger of venereal disease, which is inordinately high in these regions, and a sense of having sinned.

The white man who falls for these lures will probably be robbed, perhaps beaten and possibly murdered.

On one morning, on the roof of a squalid walkup, four white men were found strangled and stripped, their bodies thrown behind a chimney. This was the work of one prostitute whose pimp and accomplice crouched in hiding, and when each man was least likely to have his wits and caution, came up over him and choked him to death with bare hands while the woman held him helpless.

This, of course, is an extreme instance. But cases of "badger" workers are everyday occurrences; a white man is no sooner in an embarrassing position but in comes a Negro who claims to be the woman's "husband," and—usually with a weapon, but sometimes only on a threat of arrest—cleans the victim of all he has with him. There are also "panel" houses. These work by having the woman help the man take his clothing off and place it in a certain position, probably over a convenient chair. While he is concentrated on thoughts other than his watch and money, a panel slides open, a dark hand comes through and takes everything out of the pockets.

When a man has finished with such an amour, he generally feels a bit of revulsion and is eager to get out. Therefore he usually does not realize that he has been frisked and by the time he does, he is reluctant to return and is probably afraid, realizing that he has been in a thieves' den. Should he ask a policeman to go with him, he would have to explain how and why he was there in the first place. Should he return alone, he would probably get no answer at the bell, or if he did it would be with a beer bottle or a knife.

The same effect is often attained without a confederate. The woman goes through the man's clothes while he is in no frame of mind to keep his hands on his pockets. This is subtly known in Harlem as "cold finger work."

The cost of living has gone up here as it has everywhere. The price of a woman, 20 years ago, in Harlem was from 25 cents up. Today a good-looking one, especially if she is not leading a man to be skinned, has no compunction about asking $20.

Surely, the most ardent protagonist of Harlem will not challenge its predilection towards sexual and other vices.

Practically every novel and factual exposé by Negro writers and by white writers who glorify Negroes is replete with accounts of illicit relations between white men and dark girls. The Negro newspapers harp on it constantly. And if more proof is needed, contemplate the fact that the largest dance hall in Harlem was closed by the License Commissioner because it was overrun with 12-year-old Negro prostitutes; and one of the larger theatres in Harlem was closed by the License Commissioner because of indescribable orgies in the balcony during theatrical performances.

The result of these disclosures and the hundreds of muggings has been to drive the New York white element, except for an occasional and misguided drunken sailor, out of the area.

Mugging has nothing to do with sex. It is a white invention, in old Chicago days called "strongarming." The technique is for a man or woman—it is operated by both—to come up behind a man or a woman and throw an arm around the front of the throat, closing it sharply, with the elbow out. This gives an immediate condition of semi-helplessness and the defense against it is difficult because both hands are not as strong as one arm. At the same time, the mugger shoves a knee into the small of the back of the victim, further devitalizing him or her and throwing off any balance which might permit of a struggle. By this time one or more co-workers are going through the handbag or the pockets.

Often those selected by such criminals are persons who have been seen in saloons or elsewhere with valuables or sums of money worth the effort. In not a few cases, where victims have put up a struggle, they were stabbed or choked to death.

The comparatively high-class Negro cafés with entertainment which flourished during Prohibition were put out of business by a number of concurrent consequences.

The kindly, grinning, amiable and frequently obsequious Negro was disappearing. In his place came a truculent, class-conscious, race-conscious and union-conscious, embittered man or woman, resenting whites and demanding white wages.

The early clubs, with their all-night white carriage trade, their quick and friendly waiters and their low-comedy performers had to fold. Negroes working for a white employer demanded white men's pay. Negro workers insulted white patrons. The new trend decried Negroes stooping to low comedy—the calling was for dignity; no more thick red lips or prop watermelons or plantation togs. Why shouldn't they sing grand opera? Why shouldn't they play Shakespeare? They have done both, with here and there some success, often overestimated by "tolerant" critics, but there is no more Negro theatre and there is practically no Negro entertainment as it was known so long, a native American institution.

The minstrel show, which was at one time tops in popularity on our stages, was wiped out forever, far ahead of the Uncle Tom shows, which the CIO and the societies for the advancement of colored people picketed out of existence.

There are three good-sized night clubs in Harlem now. They play to very few whites, except those who regularly "mix." It may surprise many of our readers to know that in the constantly growing mingling of whites and Negroes, white women with black men are far more numerous than white men with black women.

The Harlem community accepts—though it despises —these Caucasians who cross the color line, or as it is known above 110th Street, "change their luck" or "deal in coal."

It is common knowledge that girls and women associated with night life to a certain degree have long crossed the line. These are usually dope addicts. That does not mean that many of them are not fresh and young and desirable.

From the days of earliest slavery in the United States and the West Indies, Negroes have swept away their heavy inhibitions, forgotten the burn of the lash and the clank of the shackles with an age-old drug, hashish.

Hashish was used among the ancients to stimulate armies for ruthless killing.

It has since become known as locoweed and in Harlem it is commonly called "tea," and the cigarettes made therefrom are called "reefers" or "muggles." Technically, in the United States Drug Act legislation, this weed, containing a chemical substance known as cannabine, is called marijuana.

No amount of vigilance can stamp out marijuana. It grows anywhere. The Negro chauffeur of one of the authors of this book saved enough money to buy a farm—to grow nothing but marijuana. Acres of it have been found within the city limits of New York and in its environs. It can be grown in back yards and even in window boxes and will flourish.

Because this innocent-looking weed is so prolific and so hardy, a special police class has lectured on its idiosyncrasies. The students were ordered then to keep a keen eye out and if they saw any of it to report it to a specified bureau.

Only one turned in a holler. He had discerned it on a lawn. He gave the address.

An expert was rushed there by auto. He found it, all right—it was in the front yard of a police station!

One plant, which does not occupy more than a square inch of dirt and does not require more than four times that much for nourishment will grow 100 seeds (pistilates). Crushed with the pods and leaves and rolled, that plant will make ten reefers.

The cigarettes come in three qualities—"sars-fras"—the cheapest kind, sold to thousands of school children at about two bits each; the "panatella," or "messerole," retailed at fifty cents; and the top grade, the "gungeon," which produces a voluptuous "bang," bringing as high as a dollar.

There are about 500 apartments in Harlem, known as "tea pads," set up exclusively for marijuana addicts. They are darkly lit, the colors are usually deep blue, there is a juke box or victrola with the jumpiest of jive records. An insidious incense pervades the stuffy air; windows are always closed. The walls are usually scrawled with crude nudes and pornographic sketches.

Here gather the reefer smokers for their "binge." That's the origin of the word for a drunk in modern slang. And drunk is how they get. The first few puffs create an almost painful parching of the throat. This calls for liquor to wet the whistle. The combination of marijuana and alcohol brings on a complete flight of conscience, restraint, decency and shame.

What occurs after such a debauch gets going, in a small flat, with two or three bedrooms and an assemblage of interracial participants of both sexes, will not be described here.

Broadway and theatrical women are not necessarily looser than other women. But for many years, and especially during the 20's and 30's, in vaudeville and musical revues it became the custom to introduce Negroes into companies with whites; especially Negro musicians, who undoubtedly have certain generic talents which white men cannot match.

It is a matter of long record that bandsmen rank high in the lists of narcotics users. Many of our best-known white musicians have been in public trouble over this weakness and thousands of others are known within the profession to be so inclined.

Through the combination of the mingling of Negroes who used marijuana when other dope was cheap and plentiful and still used it and could get it and had established places to smoke it as the other drugs evaporated, white women learned where they could get a "belt," a "jolt" or a "gow." Reefer-smokers are called "gowsters."

To those who are "hooked," which in the argot means they have the habit, the tea pad sessions are known as "kicking the gong around." That's the origin of this often misused bit of modern idiom. A newcomer into the fold is called a "joy popper." Occasionals or slummers who manage to crash, through a "connection," are called "RFD gowsters." When one becomes so habituated that marijuana is an incurable obsession, "the monkey is riding on his (or her) back."

Recently there has been a steady infiltration of society, bohemian and co-ed recruits among white females who go to Harlem for its lurid pleasures. Many women in the professional labor movement have heard the call to prove openly that they are broadminded. Many avowed Communists all but push themselves on the Negroes and it is a tenet of the party line in New York City that white women must go out of their way to mingle with the colored comrades.

Not all these mix hashish with their politics. But sex is considered a mandatory gesture of complete conversion.

Ironically enough, while all this over-emphasis on tolerance, equality and the brotherhood of man has taken on the magnitude of big business, the Negroes are decidedly anti-Semitic, and Jew-baiting is a constant maneuver in organized and disorganized form. Certain Negro gangs, mostly composed of zoot-suited teen-agers, make a regular practice of it and call it "Jew-hunting." They find fertile ground for it in the nearby Bronx and set off on expeditions to beat up Jewish children going to and from school.

To understand the Negro as a gangster one must look with accusing eyes at the white toughs who so long terrorized the Negroes.

Wherever the blacks poured across a street to take up new habitations that would accommodate the constant influx from the South and widening opportunities for those already in the North, seeking to escape from their hideous encirclement under unspeakable conditions, they were fought and often killed by hooligans from such old mobs as the Hancocks, the Irish Dukes, the Rainbows and the Goat Hill Hoodlums, who originated in the days of Irish squatter possession of Lexington Avenue and west, north of 96th Street.

The Negroes defended themselves the best they could, and under the guidance of grownup "captains and war counsellors," as they are still known, they organized what now constitutes about 75 gangs in upper Manhattan. They run from 25 to 40 and some to 200.

Among the principal Negro gangs are the Sabres, the Socialists, the Chancellors, the Buccaneers, the Copians, the Barons and the Slicksters.

Their activities now range from fighting each other for the pure love of bloodshed (called "rumbles") to highway robbery. Often fights are faked so that in the confusion and the crowd a quick job of larceny is inconspicuous.

The Chancellors, a strict organization with rank and titles, according to age, strength, bravado and accomplishments, is typical. The groups run progressively up from Tiny Tims to Midgets to Juniors to Seniors. Each class takes orders from the one above and all are as strictly ruled and disciplined as were the Czar's Cossacks, by their war counsellors, known as "bigs."

Not the least of their power is in their auxiliaries, girls ranging from 12 years up, who start as Sub-debs and graduate to become Debs. They are usually the mistresses of the Seniors. Their roles are important before, during and after acts of violence.

By police regulations, only females may search females. The Debs and Sub-debs are usually from 50 to 500 feet behind the warriors. They carry the weapons. Should there be a sudden police charge, the girls evaporate in all directions and the men are found unarmed. But the moment the first fist flies, they rush in and slip the tools to the Chancellors. Very often they join in the fight with them and punch, bite and stab, and are quite as vicious as the males.

The weapons, featuring the switch-blade spring knife which is the Harlem standby, also run to first-rate shooting arms and homemade guns which are converted from lengths of tubing. Billies, sword-canes and ice-picks are standard equipment. The harmless-looking souvenir toy bats sold at the ball parks, which can crack a skull at a single swipe, are regularly employed.

Developed from self-defense against the whites, the lust for battle and pillage has become a menace to the respectable Negroes. No colored gangster will stoop to work. Once he belongs, he must make his living with his fists and weapons or he must have a woman support him. Harlem is probably the only community on earth where the women earn more money than do the men. Thousands of them are employed as servants and others do well plying less savory trades. It is regarded as manly and superior for a man to be kept, and to prove his masculinity he is expected occasionally to beat his woman to show her who is master.

The younger thugs, who have not reached that lofty estate, but who must not attempt to be Alger boys, bluntly live by robbery. In some sections a Negro boy or girl not belonging to a powerful gang scarcely dares leave home with a nickel. In addition to being despoiled, they are frequently manhandled.

As a result, many Negro families have sent their children to New Jersey and Long Island and even back south of the Mason and Dixon Line because of the intolerable abuses from their own race.

In fact, Congressman Powell, whose district comprises Harlem, and his actress wife spend most of their time on Long Island. Powell, a light-skinned, but professional Negro and bleeding heart, and Mrs. Powell—Hazel Scott—ride in a chauffeur-driven Cadillac limousine. Miss Scott was cited as a left-winger by the Un-American Activities committee.

On his own statement, a 13-year-old Negro boy, who held up a white schoolteacher at gun point and was caught while fleeing, a clasp knife in his hand and his .32-calibre revolver in his belt, was a member of the Purple Cross gang, with a hangout at 114th Street and St. Nicholas Avenue.

He was ambitious to join the Turks, a gang of older boys. He was told he would have to prove he was tough enough. The Turk leaders gave him the gun and told him to pull a stick-up—"then come back and we'll see about taking you in."

One juvenile Harlem gang has another test—before a tyro can be accepted as a full member, he must commit a rape!

The Negroes took merciless punishment in the big depression. And the recovery was slow for them. By 1940 they were angry and sullen. Then hell broke loose, fomented by meddlesome agitators of both races. A bloody and paralyzing race riot exploded.

The police, suddenly allowed to wade in with night-sticks, finished it quickly. But the causes could not be clubbed down. The resentment and bitterness went underground, to emerge through influences described above, but with few flare-ups because the whites virtually quit going to Harlem.

For months, no taxi driver would take whites to Harlem destinations, and some even refused to drive through the district. Even today few white hackmen will take you to a Harlem number or answer a hail in that region.

The muggings and the stick-ups soon began to slop far over the borders and today the extent of Negro crime in all the boroughs scandalizes the decent elements of the race. White men have the money. And since they no longer come up to be taken, the goons spread to greener fields.

Lait and Mortimer have set up above only a camera-eye fragment of their long experience and what they learned first-hand in courts, police stations, and day and night contacts with every class and phase of New York's metropolitan manifestations.

They have eaten in Harlem hideaways and imbibed at Harlem's beehive bars. They have had the confidence of Negro detectives, who are too ashamed of the behavior of some of their people to gloss it over.

This chapter will reform nothing. It was written with no such intent. Its sole function is to inform, and the information should serve as a warning.

Harlem is no place for joy hoppers or joy poppers. Outside of the few white people who have business there and who are familiarly recognized, the sight of a white person in the black precincts brings one of several instant reactions:

If it's a white man "on the make," the Negroes are infuriated, though the dregs of their own women are there to solicit him; if a white woman is seen, she is either a tramp or a nut with a yen for colored men, and though plenty of colored men are willing, Harlem looks on her as a pariah and an intruder; if a white man and wife walk the avenues, looking curiously here and there, they are peepers who regard the Negroes as the zoo visitors do the exhibits in their cages; if white men go to the worst parts of Harlem to get drunk—God help them.

The old days are over. Gawkers and the idly curious who don't know their Harlem may gamble their very lives. Therefore, the gospel of this chapter is: If you haven't legitimate business there—

Stay Away From Harlem!

12. AND YE TOOK ME IN!

DURING THE last 12 years and growing every year, there has descended on Manhattan Island like a locust plague an influx of Puerto Ricans.

They arrive now frequently at the rate of 2,000 a month and there are today more than 600,000 natives of the island (one authority calculates 710,000) cramped, some 30 in one cold-water flat, mostly in one section of this great island, the whole of which is much smaller than theirs in area.

One of every four persons born in this generation in Puerto Rico is in New York; one of every 13 New Yorkers is a Puerto Rican.

Referring to these Caribbean wards of the nation as a plague is not prompted by prejudice, anger or careless use of phraseology.

Puerto Ricans were not born to be New Yorkers. They are mostly crude farmers, subject to congenital tropical diseases, physically unfitted for the northern climate, unskilled, uneducated, non-English-speaking and almost impossible to assimilate and condition for healthful and useful existence in an active city of stone and steel.

It would be tragic enough if the sorry results were the consequences only of desperate displaced persons fleeing to a haven of hope from the circumscribed possibilities of their birthplace.

But the story is far more sordid. A majority of these

people were lured here deliberately, because, as American citizens, they can vote. They are a power behind ex-Congressman Vito Marcantonio, until recently the only American Labor Party member of the House, who rules the wretched section into which a majority of the 600,000 have poured from leaky ships and from miserable chartered planes which are almost beyond description.

The Puerto Ricans at this moment are costing New York City $12,000,000 a year in relief. There is no residence-period requirement, that having been knocked out during the LaGuardia administration, when Marcantonio's word could wipe out law.

Not only are many of these Puerto Ricans on relief within an hour after their feet land on a dock or a secondary airport, but some are already booked on the dole in advance, while they are in the air or on the water.

Until recently Marcantonio maintained a full-time representative in the office of the Welfare Department, whose business it was to get his constituents not only registered on the rolls but also provided with fat and flowing allowances, using broadly every channel created for emergency cases. Now it is done surreptitiously, but still done.

For voting, the law requires one year in the state, four months in the county, one month in the district. But it is impossible to check, even if the holdover handout officials would want to. The Puerto Ricans all look alike, their names all sound alike and if an inspector calls in one of the swarming flats in the teeming tenements, nobody speaks English.

Travel agencies whip up the movement through agents in Puerto Rico. The newspapers and the billboards and even signs stuck beside the dirt roads of the remote regions shout with bargain rates as low as $20 for a flight to New York; ship transportation is sometimes even cheaper than that.

Very few Puerto Ricans at home have or ever have had $20. But the money seems to come from somewhere.

Privately, these poverty-numbed, naïve natives are sold a bill of the tremendous possibilities in the great New York which they have seen in the movies and in the patent insides of their local sheets. They are told that here fortunes await many and the rest can quickly go on relief for sums undreamt-of by them or their fathers' fathers.

The result is a sullen, disappointed, disillusioned mass of people, alien to everything that spells New York. The children quickly learn to resent the fact that, though they are Americans, they are foreigners who cannot speak the language and are thus teased and humiliated in schools and on the streets.

Because they are dark of complexion, they are commonly classified as Negroes and share a large portion of the unfortunate prejudice which still bedevils non-Caucasians, even in a community as broad-minded as New York.

Few can obtain employment, though Marcantonio and a few other politicians place them, to a conspicuous disproportion, in minor public jobs, in hospitals, prisons, public works and other institutions where no skills and no English are required.

The youths of both sections run wild. They take on the vilest habits of their surroundings, and the description elsewhere in this book of conditions in Harlem apply very generally to the sections where the Puerto Ricans have swarmed.

As in the case of Harlem, the Puerto Ricans are concentrated in a small area but do not entirely make that their pleasure ground.

During the last two years there has been a steady flow toward Broadway, until the corners in the lower 50's are crowded day and night with zoot-suited men who hang around the riffraff of the amusement centers and so behave that it has long been necessary to post extra police south of Columbus Circle, around the clock.

They soon become marijuana addicts, throng into cheap and crowded dives which cater to their trade, and many become violent criminals with gun and knife. Many of them are dope-peddlers while on relief.

In their own district the children are natural cop-haters, throw stones at prowl cars and drop bricks from the roofs on uniformed policemen.

There are no tougher saloons in Marseilles, Shanghai, Port Said or Panama City than those which seethe with these island immigrants. 108th Street and Second Avenue is the headquarters of the international dope racket.

The crime rate is stupendous and it is increasing and spreading.

One General Sessions judge who had just finished a six-week trial calendar of criminal cases covering the entire borough of Manhattan reported to one of your authors that more than 40 per cent of convictions during that term had been of Puerto Ricans, of whom 2 per cent were born on the United States mainland.

The disease statistics are even more shocking.

Not a few of the natives are cursed with tuberculosis and syphilis before they arrive; a Puerto Rican leper was discovered not long ago. But once they are here, the venereal incidence is marked with a rapid rise, due to association with low prostitutes, with the result that a random health inspection of 1,000 Puerto Rican males between the ages of 15 and 40 revealed 80 per cent infected.

The conditions which cause these frightful statistics are largely parallel to those which afflict the Negroes, but the Puerto Ricans are harmed even more by these conditions because they are strangers, because they have not come of their own free will, like adventurers of courage and enterprise from other lands, who brave regions beyond their horizon to fight for their opportunities.

Most of these are not only outmatched in every battle of life in the fastest and biggest city in the world, but they were far behind in their own unhappy land before they left, and that was why they left.

The callous exploitation of these weaklings is one of the dirtiest crimes in the long and shameful record of practical American politics. None knows better than those who have primed and prompted and financed the exodus, what they are doing to these victims and what they are doing to the city where they bring them in gutted one-motor planes, sitting on bucket seats, sometimes so crowded that many stand all the way, air-sick and already homesick.

The sight of one of these outmoded flying cattle boats, long since discarded by the government services and regular transport lines, is horrifying and nauseating.

The pilgrims are dropped off at Newark or small private landing places, carrying bundles and babies and the weight of fear and sorrow, through which the gleam of new hope cannot penetrate.

They are marched in and carried in dilapidated buses directly to the filthy, shrieking, miserable rookeries where housing has long been exhausted. This means that each new arrival will be shoe-horned into already jammed, unsanitary, indecent lodgings, to sleep on the floor or even in a hallway.

The relief figures look good and they should, because they are designedly excessive. But prices are high and before these strangers arrive the sharks are waiting and smacking their lips.

And so they constitute not only a horde unfitted for the new habitat, but they quickly become resentful under the hostile conditions, so different from the utopia which smooth-tongued agents painted to people who had never been off the island on which they were born.

Not only that frame of mind, but public support, with a tremendous factor of idleness, proximity to the regions of lowest vice and highest crime, easy opportunity to mingle in the swirl of the unwashed underworld, rapidly perverts them.

They pick up the bad habits of those with whom they are forced to associate, and these they amplify with the enthusiasm of untutored islanders for illegitimate revelry and dissipation.

Merchants of every form of dope, vice and alcohol await them eagerly with merchandise within their means.

Finding themselves unable physically, mentally or financially to compete, they turn to guile and wile and the steel blade, the traditional weapon of the sugarcane cutter, mark of their blood and heritage.

New York, of course, is not easily pushed around and turns on them, which makes them more bitter and more belligerent, which brings upon them heavier punishment, which makes them uglier, and thus a constant and increasing spiral of hatred spins around these hundreds of thousands.

Some manage to straggle back. But it is an established fact that the city holds and fascinates and imprisons those who have once felt the magic of its embrace.

Columbia University made a survey of the situation. The governor of Puerto Rico put through an appropriation for the island legislature to run down the facts. The Welfare Department of the city and state have thrown up their hands in helpless surrender to this

modern scandal, entirely unforeseen only a few years
ago, though Puerto Ricans have had free access without passport to the United States since 1898.

The City Welfare Council, in a sympathetic report
glossing over much of the situation, nevertheless described *"back yards piled high with garbage," also one
block so infested with drunks, marijuana smokers,
brawlers, holdup men and insulters of women that decent citizens and even the police deliberately avoid it.*

So, this chapter is not merely an observation about
a portion of Manhattan Island. It is an exposition of a
situation which will echo in the halls of Congress and
will write its own pages in the history of the nation,
because, as has been pointed out, it is far from static;
in every phase it is growing and the sorry end is nowhere in sight.

13. UP IN CENTRAL PARK

*M*ICHAEL TODD, a theatrical producer who hails from Chicago, made a valuable contribution to the unorthodox history of Manhattan with the long-run hit musical play, *Up in Central Park,* later made into a movie.

Those fortunate enough to have seen this gay operetta may remember references to a crooked land-grab in connection with the building of the park, which packed the coffers of many Tammanyites of the day.

We have thousands of acres of parks in New York; a world-famed zoo and botanical gardens in the Bronx. None, however, can compare with Central Park, a jewel of emerald green in a rectangular setting of mansions and museums and skyscrapers.

But Central Park is not the chaste oasis its verdure and placid lakes might imply.

The prime spot for a pick-up (if you're not hoity-toity) is the Central Park Mall, during the summer, though Riverside Drive runs a close second—if you're a sailor.

Some years ago, the beneficent city fathers inaugurated a program of free dances in Central Park. They were primarily designed for young men and women of the poorer districts.

They also drew degenerates, rapists and wolves.

It's standard practice there to ask any gal to dance

and it doesn't seem to matter what color you are or she is.

Many fallen sisters—and very reasonably—take advantage of this frolic on the green to ply their avocation under police protection.

But the amateurs—especially the bobby sox juvenile delinquents—give them unethical competition.

Friendly bushes, in the darkness, provide privacy (of a sort) for a necking party. But those who stray too far from the well-lighted Mall invite serious danger.

Lurking in the park are all manner of anti-social characters, from footpads to vicious sex-maniacs. Blood-curdling crimes are common.

The police cannot patrol every foot of the big expanse of the park, though at times they have had remarkable success in keeping crime at a minimum by dressing a couple of boyish detectives in women's clothes and turning them loose on the scum.

The place is, of course, a happy hunting ground for psychopathic and physical irregulars, who find it an excellent layout to strike up acquaintances with others of their kind.

The southwest corner of the park, at Columbus Circle, has been pre-empted by Negro homos. The north border, Cathedral Parkway (110th) is alive with wicked wenches.

And yet, graceful old Central Park is one of the most beautiful places remaining in this modernist crazy world.

Its lights, architecture and landscaping retain the pre-rococo charm of the last century.

But the old Central Park Casino is gone, a victim of the leveling-down process of the dictatorship of the rabble.

Here, in a charming building surrounded by trees and the greensward, was one of New York's showspots of the hectic 20's where society and café society dined, danced and broke the dry law.

As Jimmy Walker's night city hall (he rarely arose in time to visit the official one), the casino attracted the cream—and the sour milk—of New York officialdom and gangdom. Its prices were outrageous, but its food divine, its liquor bona fide and its dance music memorable.

LaGuardia, darling of the déclassé, elected in 1933 on a platform of revenge and revulsion against civilized living, made the destruction of the Central Park Casino the first major issue in his campaign of social nihilism. He said the land was needed for a playground.

No sooner was the casino leveled than he found an excuse to open another dining and dance pavilion in the park, for concessionaires more friendly to his regime.

To do this he destroyed the historic old sheepfold, where generations of city kids learned about nature watching the grazing lambs, and turned the building into a cabaret called "The Tavern on the Green."

Though its prices are not as astronomical as those imposed by the mourned casino, they are still too high for New York's millions of low-income citizens—the voters LaGuardia said the park was for.

Tucked away on a crosswalk in the 60's is a crazy little carousel, circa last century. Here the kids ride the merry-go-round to a tinkly, wheezy calliope playing the same tunes heard there by Teddy Roosevelt. Here is one of New York's most delightful nooks for romance.

You still find the hackies at 59th Street and Fifth Avenue, the last of their kind in the country. Best time to ride is after 4 A.M., when the motor traffic in the park has come to a standstill and you have the place all to yourself in a barouche or hansom.

If your doll still holds out, after winding slowly through leaf-covered roads, to the tune of the horse's cloppety-clop, wake up the driver and order him right to the morgue. She's dead.

14. NEW YORK'S DORMITORIES

WE ARE going to go statistical on you for a few paragraphs and tell you something about the size of greater New York and the parts of it which you'll probably never get to see—and you don't know how lucky you are, at that.

The population of the incorporated city of New York is approximately 8,000,000, one out of every 17 in the land. One of every 10 Americans lives in New York's metropolitan district, which includes the overlapping areas of Westchester and Nassau counties, New Jersey and Connecticut, within 45-minutes commuting distance from Times Square.

Perhaps one of every 100 persons on earth—20,000,000—live within 100 miles of New York, are employed here, or are frequent visitors for business or pleasure.

Manhattan Island, which is the county of New York, is the core of all this, but actually it is only second in population of the city's boroughs, having about 2,000,000 permanent residents. The balance of the metropolis' huge population sleeps elsewhere.

Brooklyn, approaching 3,000,000, ranks by itself the second largest city in the nation; in area it sprawls all over the map, a maddening maze of crazy streets apparently without beginning or end.

The unwary visitor to Brooklyn who asks a policeman how to get somewhere usually is directed to return to Manhattan and start all over again. The natives don't know their way about in this gigantic and illogical patchwork.

The incorporated city of Greater New York, which was born in 1898, when the independent municipality of Brooklyn merged with Manhattan, consists of five boroughs, each coextensive with a county.

They are:

Borough	County	Pop. 1950	Rank
Manhattan...............	New York	1,938,551	2
Brooklyn................	Kings	2,720,238	1
Bronx..................	Bronx	1,444,903	4
Queens.................	Queens	1,546,316	3
Richmond...............	Richmond	191,015	5

Brooklyn and Queens each occupy the westernmost end of Long Island. Manhattan is located on its island. Richmond occupies all Staten Island. The much-maligned Bronx is the sole borough on the mainland of the United States.

Richmond, historically and geographically a part of New Jersey, from which it is separated by only a narrow kill spanned by a bridge, is five miles from Manhattan, half an hour by ferry. The other boroughs are all connected with each other by land borders, bridges or tunnels.

Considerable confusion exists concerning New York's borough system, because it is the only city in the world including more than one county in its corporate limits.

The counties are not called boroughs. They merely happen to have the same geographic boundaries as the boroughs. The five counties in New York City are, like all other counties in the state, political subdivisions of the State of New York. The boroughs, on the other hand, are political subdivisions of the City of New York.

Each of New York's five counties has its own District (State's) Attorney and courts.

The borough governments, presided over by presidents who are their bailiwicks' representatives in the upper chamber of the municipal legislative body, exist merely for the purpose of superintending local improvements such as street repairs, etc.

Several tomes could be and have been written about Brooklyn, a place which, for some reason, always elicits guffaws when mentioned.

Brooklyn, with its Dodgers, is the most hysterical baseball community in the nation. It also embraces Flatbush, the Gowanus Canal, the fabled tree, a very old and snooty social set, in addition to the worst murderers of the English language north of the Mason and Dixon line.

Though most of Brooklyn's millions work and play in Manhattan, the borough is exceedingly provincial. It has many shopping districts, with fine stores, several popular-priced night clubs and a number of large theatres. Once a try-out spot for legit shows, which were also road showed in Brooklyn after their Broadway runs, Brooklyn, like many other large communities, has become fleshless. In olden days the Metropolitan Opera company appeared there—at the Brooklyn Academy of Music—every Tuesday during the season.

Both authors of this book are New York newspaper-men. Yet neither has been in Brooklyn six times in 20 years, except to go to Coney Island, and that is a place one seldom visits any more.

The Coney Island you can see isn't what it was, and we wouldn't advise a trip there unless you are an anti-quarian searching for rare remnants of a kaleidoscopic used-to-be. Broads who stroll the boardwalk, while often easy, usually have housemaid's knee.

The air, despite the good zestful salt sea breeze, reeks with the acrid smoke of potato knishes, garlic and frying frankfurters.

Time was when Coney's transgressions were crimson and its sinners wore silks and sables.

On the beach front, and at the adjoining Manhattan and Sheepshead beaches, were fine hotels, race tracks and fabled clubs and residences.

Mustached sports and their high-rolling ladies drank and diced, waded and swam and disappeared in pairs.

Those great levelers, the subway and the auto, which brought Coney within a dime of any part of New York, soon leveled Coney. The dime became its sym-bol. Luna Park is gone, destroyed by fire and never rebuilt.

Steeplechase, owned by the Tilyous, related by mar-riage to Brooklyn's once ruling family, the McCooeys, has the roller coaster and nut house field practically to itself, though independent operators on Surf Avenue and the Midway, who pay no park rental fee, offer some competition.

Incidentally, the first roller coaster in the world is still in operation at Coney.

The zenith of the Coney season is the annual Mardi Gras, shortly after Labor Day, modeled after New Orleans' gala event, with local variations and no improvements.

The residents of the other boroughs, like the inhabitants of Brooklyn, are chiefly concerned with sleeping and breeding. If you find these a contradiction in terms, you don't know what they can do in the Bronx and Queens.

PART TWO

THE PEOPLE
(Confidential!)

15. THE MINX IN MINKS

(For Gals Only)

THIS IS the Enchanted City where fables and sables come true and dreams have substance, sometimes. This is the magic spot where gentlemen pay the rent for terraced apartments hanging high over the river and jalopies turn into Rolls-Royces.

Every year they come here: the little gals from farms and villages, inland whistle-stops and, now again, foreign lands. They come here, breathlessly and hopefully, in search of fame and fortune.

The men they left behind were grease-station monkeys, cow manicurists, soda jerks and coal miners. Here they seek men whose pants match their coats, who stand when a lady comes to the table, who know the difference between a filet mignon and filet de sole, and can even pronounce same.

But they don't always find them.

You, reading this, may be one of the dolls bound for New York to take it over. Or you may be a perfectly prissy schoolteacher on a two-week vacation, but with a secret and ineffable hankering to know more about the things the movies mustn't show. Or maybe you are a lady buyer, coming to the fall showings; or a wife, who, left alone by her husband, doesn't want to be by others.

The same tips go for all:

Do not come to Gotham unless you have round-trip fare. If you intend to seek coin or a career here (or just a job) do not come at all unless you have enough to keep you for four months and are insulated against a city that can say no in any language.

Do not come to New York in answer to a solicitation, personal or by mail, for a job. If anyone comes to your home town with offers of good positions in Manhattan, turn him over to the police. Odds are he's an advance man for a call house.

Do not come unless you have friends here already, for it can be a mighty lonesome place. If you are an easy mixer and don't care, you can eliminate the requirement for friends.

Do not come to New York for a visit ALONE. There is practically nothing a girl can do here without an escort, or at least without the company of another girl, except ride the dirty subways and stare at the obelisk.

If you can't dragoon a man of your own you are just out of luck. Even the escort services have been banned by law.

But remember, New Yorkers seldom try for pickups on the streets, in buses or lobbies. Any girl who responds to a raw come-on may be smiling back at a handsome dick on the vice squad.

However, it is considered o.k. (at your own risk, of course, not ours) to respond to "It's a nice evening, isn't it?" at dance halls, at free dances, bathing beaches, swimming pools, cocktail bars, church and YMCA socials.

Also, on the street (but only if you or he may be walking a dog and one or the other stops to admire it).

*   *   *

Most night clubs and cocktail bars do not admit or permit unescorted women after 10 P.M.

(At this writing the City Council and State Legislature are considering bills to ban unescorted women at bars at any time.)

Never talk to strangers in theatres, on subways or in other public places.

You may nod to him in a hotel if you both live there and have seen each other before.

DO NOT walk in Central Park, or other parks AFTER DARK, even if escorted.

*   *   *

CONFESSIONS OF A CAUTIOUS CUTIE:

Smart Gotham gals don't keep diaries. If what goes into 'em is unimportant, why bother? If it's secret stuff, never put it in writing.

Gals who pass out after five (or 55) drinks should wear identification bracelets with name and address—especially when on a first date with a gent who may not know where to deliver the body. In no event should dolls who can't handle their liquor step out with men who can't carry theirs. Who takes whom home?

When entering a night club, a smart gal doesn't stop at the bar to greet every drunk, just to show her escort she's a doll-about-town.

Do not use cheap perfume when night clubbing (or at any time).

Don't invite gents who call for you into your apartment. Have them meet you below. If they once get in, they may decide they'll stay a while, smoke your cigarettes, drink all your liquor, raid your ice box, and then if you won't give in, they won't buy you dinner.

*   *   *

Few Gotham glamor gals are home-grown. Our gals don't go in much for show business and modeling. Those professionals you see on the street and in the night clubs almost all come from out of town.

The deep South—Texas, Oklahoma, Georgia and Florida—towns like Scranton, Pa., and West Coast points, contribute most of our flashy frails.

For a long time, during the war, our source of supply was cut off, when the gals made more money at home in defense work or as waitresses than they could expect to begin with in the expensive-to-live-in metropolis.

But in days before that, there was no horizon at home for a good-looker with ambitions.

They hitchhiked, rumbled in by bus, train and plane. The more fortunate became models or show girls. One of a thousand went on to fame and fortune in Hollywood or acquired a millionaire, in or out of wedlock.

But the reward for the lucky ones is so great that for every failure a dozen new, young, starry-eyed twists come to town.

147

The case of Mary Stuart, of Tulsa, Okla., is typical.

It is one of the stories that could only happen on Broadway.

The chief characters:

Joe Pasternak, famed movie producer and discoverer of Deanna Durbin; his wife, the former Dorothy Darrell, who was a chorus girl Cinderella, and Mary Stuart, the 19-year-old beaut from out West.

But let us start from the beginning. Destiny stopped in Tulsa and pointed his long, bony finger straight at New York. Mary took the hint.

That day she shoved off. Lacking the fare, she thumbed her way. She had no difficulty flagging rides. For Mary, as we've told you, is a beaut. She has soft brown hair and a figure curved in the right places to accentuate all her loveliness—all 118 pounds and five-feet-five of it.

So she had no difficulty finding work here, as a model by day and as a photo girl in the Grill Room of the Hotel Roosevelt at night.

Into the Grill one night came Pasternak and his own lovely wife, accepting an invitation extended by Guy Lombardo, maestro at the spot.

Miss Stuart, hotly hoping she'd be seen by a Hollywood mogul, had been fired from the photo concession the day before.

But Destiny hadn't been; it was still working.

Through the voice of one of the musicians in Lombardo's band, whom she knew well, Destiny whispered to her that Pasternak had a reservation for that evening.

For a few bucks, Mary fixed it up with another photo girl and paraded past the Pasternaks with the camera.

Mrs. Pasternak saw Mary first, remarked about her beauty to Joe.

Mary, near their table, began to hum in tune to the music.

Pasternak addressed her. "Do you sing?" he asked.

Mary modestly admitted she did—a little.

Pasternak asked to hear her. Mary was unprepared. He said he might leave town next day. So he asked Lombardo to let her try a number with the orchestra.

When Mary got there, she didn't even bother to talk the song over with the piano player. Confidentially, she had rehearsed it with him earlier in the day, framing up the whole thing for Pasternak's visit.

She sang two songs.

Pasternak later admitted she was no world-beater as a thrush. And he had caught on to the game.

"I decided that any girl with that much gall had a hell of a chance in pictures," he told Lombardo.

So he signed her to a contract—that night—without a screen test.

Pasternak, who also discovered the charming and talented Kathryn Grayson, has flirted successfully with Fate more than once. His own stunning wife was, before meeting him, a chorus girl who, in her teens, had been around Broadway so long she was considered "an old face" and practically washed up.

So she joined a touring line of rumba dancers. Far from New York, Pasternak saw her in a night club, asked to meet her, whipped out his fountain pen and a contract and shipped her to Universal, at which studio he then labored.

Dorothy appeared in minor roles in several pictures.

Then she interrupted her promising career to marry her discoverer—a dear friend of her ex-sweetie, Harry Richman, whom she had once followed to London only to be deported by the British authorities because she had neither passport nor money.

But, if any guy says to you, "Honey, you oughtta be in pichures. Let's go up to my room and talk it over," *DON'T*. That is *not* the way to get in pictures. That's the way to get in trouble!

16. GUYS AND PEARLS

(For Men Only)

DON'T be a cluck!

Sure, New York is the home of Tiffany and Cartier, Bonwit and Saks, Milgrim and Bergdorf-Goodman.

But Gotham gals don't flop for saps, simps or retail buyers.

They'll take everything you've got to give 'em—and take you for what you haven't got.

But the more you shower on them, the more they'll laugh at you—while cheating with another.

Of course, if you're only in town for a few days or a few weeks, and you have a penchant for orchidaceous glamor dolls, you've got to kick in and hand out—handsomely.

But don't overdo it. Be careful how you do it.

None but hustlers are for sale. So, whatever you give, make it look like a gift of appreciation for the pleasure, instead of a bribe or fee.

* * *

O.K. You are a lonesome gent in New York, looking for company, and where are you going to find *her?* Of course, we don't know what your taste is—whether you like them little or tall, blonde or brunette, breezily hep or delightfully dumb.

But, let us warn you, Manhattan is mined for a lonely guy.

Best policed city in the world, despite an occasional scandal, there's little opportunity for street pick-ups here, and the quality of what you could pick up is so inferior, you'd be cheated.

New York's cafés and clubs are forbidden by law to employ hostesses or "B" girls, and a police regulation bans mixing between female entertainers and guests.

This rule is so strictly enforced in the big, first-class night clubs, that the members of the casts are required to enter and leave the premises by the stage door.

A friend of ours, a newspaperman, was married to a red-headed hoofer in a Broadway night club. Because of the variance in their hours, the only opportunity they had to visit socially with one another was between shows at her club.

One night, while she was sitting with her husband, the cops raided the place and took up its license. The offense: A female entertainer "mixing" with a guest.

When it was explained to the police that the couple —if not respectable—were at least respectably married, the flat-feet scratched their heads. After prolonged and profound thought, they refused to drop the charges.

"The law says no gals can sit with guys," they stated. "It don't say nothing here about no husbands."

The club was suspended for 10 days.

Some of the taxi dance halls on Broadway employ broads who will dance with you for a dime a dance (and up) plus tip. They are not supposed to make dates with you, and you won't want to anyway, unless you are desperate or dizzy.

If they do date you, you've got to wait until the place closes, at one, or later, then meet them elsewhere than at the dance hall.

(But where are you going with them, during the hotel shortage?)

Turn to Chapter 33 for how to meet friends.

INSIDE STUFF: Many smaller night clubs, especially those on side streets and in Greenwich Village, cheat. Some headwaiters have been known to introduce strangers for a stiff tip. But if you sit out with the tramps in these places, count your drinks, watch your check—and better check your watch.

* * *

BEWARE of steerers. If a stranger in the street or hotel lobby or a cab driver asks you if you want to meet a gal, shake your head hard. Odds are he is a runner for a clip joint.

* * *

WISDOM OF A WHITE WAY WOLF:

Don't date a late-dater unless you are her late date. (Late-dater: a doll who ducks out on her dinner date at midnight to meet another guy—usually a musician.)

Three funny gags that make 'em laugh are worth more than three hours of romantic salesmanship.

Get yourself a big, fierce-looking hound and walk him around the block. Not only is there a free-masonry between all pooch-lovers, male and female . . . but plenty of soft little cuties will stop to admire the brute. Then . . .

Most girls are now too smart for the "ya oughta be in pichures" hokum, but no doll can stand off a guy who "breaks her down." Insults far oftener than flattery bust barriers on Broadway.

Never trust a gal any farther than you can throw a trap-drummer.

Common courtesy demands that if your doll airs you, she rates one day to return. (Unless you have to catch a train home that day—then give her two hours.) If she doesn't show up, find a stand-in. Census bureau says there will be 750,000 more does than stags in this postwar world.

When you take a likely candidate to the Stork or El Morocco, don't try to impress her with your friendship with big shots by introducing her to a movie star or millionaire playboy. She'll probably end up with him —instead of you.

But if she rhapsodizes about a good-looking guy or celeb at another table, go and bring him over and tell him in front of her that your little friend goes for him. She'll be terribly embarrassed.

(Confessions of a Cautious Cutie: Yes, but she'll slip him her phone number, too.)

If you get your dates mixed up and end up with two Little Red Riding Hoods on the same party, don't explain. Smile in a superior way and let the pigeons fight over you—not you over them.

Never enthuse to a fellow wolf about your latest conquest—unless you're trying to lose her.

If you are with a new pretty, tip the headwaiter NOT to give you a ringside table in full view of the other wolves.

Do not let her dance with your pals. Let them dig their own. Be a good fellow, but not that good.

Don't introduce her at all if you can get out of it.

Never pan your pal to your doll and surely don't tell her he's a bad egg with women or a quick-change lover. If you do, you'll find your femme so interested, she'll turn flipflops for him.

When a date stands you up, never give her another tumble, though her alibi about rushing her sick mamma to the hospital or getting an emergency call from the casting office sounded bullet-proof. What undoubtedly happened was that her secret heart throb got back in town unexpectedly.

When you book a babe, have her meet you wherever you'll be. Only chumps wait for dames at stage doors or pick them up at their hotels. Don't be one.

* * *

WARNING:

Do not start fights in night clubs. If you think you have a legitimate beef, take your complaint to the manager. If he won't listen to you, the cops or your lawyer will. But don't start swinging. You can't win even if you are a football player, a pug, or pack a rod. You can't whip a bartender who swings a bung-starter. If you can, there's a heavy-handed bouncer, a couple of captains and a wedge of waiters waiting to show you who's boss. If they keep hands off, they'll slip you a mickey finn—and you'll wish you had never been born.

17. GLAMOR PUSSES

NEW YORK has the most beautiful bimbos on earth, and it will amuse you to learn few of them come from New York.

The authors know the buying power of their territory, and one of their ways of paying their rent is selling books.

Yet, slaves to the verities, they must say—sadly, it is true—that if you want a rollicking time with a tootsie, avoid the Bronx and Brooklyn entries.

That is, of course, a generalization. There MAY be some pretty home-grown ones. But we can't find any. Don't say we haven't tried. In the interests of science, natch, we have pursued research. But when we find one worth intensive study, we find she's from Texas, Florida, Oklahoma, Georgia, California or Quebec. Canadian chicks can be fun. But the gals who do best, and by "best" we mean what gals do best, usually come from below the Mason and Dixon line.

The proportion of pretty out-of-towners is higher than the home-bred, because New York gets the pick of the crop from everywhere else.

The homely ones stay home, marry the neighbor's son and raise pigs, chickens and brats.

The pretty pigeons get fed up on louts in lumberjackets and hit out for Life.

So the imports are pretty, whereas the home output is pretty merely in the normal proportion, which is low.

It is worth noting that, once a doll gets the title of Glamor Puss, it adheres to her for life, a-la a British order of knighthood. Some of our more famous GPs are long past the age of consent, yet they continue to make front pages, collect husbands or boy friends and costly gifts.

An example is Peggy Hopkins Joyce, born Margaret Upton, daughter of a Virginia barber, who recently acquired a seventh spouse and who is working on her eighth. She long carried on a highly publicized feud with Mabel Boll, so-called "Queen of Diamonds," daughter of a Rochester pub-keeper, on the dimensions of their gem collections.

The feud between Peggy and Mabel dated back to when they were both in the sizzling set that made headquarters at old Bustanoby's. Others in that crowd included Lillian Loraine and the Dolly Sisters.

Peggy's sweetheart then gave her a diamond ring. It was a shabby little stone, scarcely over a carat, but it was Peggy's first diamond and it gave her far more of a thrill than many of the brooches and bracelets she was to amass later. Its effect on her friend Mabel was remarkable.

Scientists will tell you that the passion for possessing precious stones is as old as recorded history. It is like a potent drug that fires the blood and flames a desire that knows no rest. So it was with Mabel. Years later she said:

"I thought it was the most beautiful stone in the world. I used to admire it by the hour and beg Peggy to let me wear it sometimes. I never hoped to own anything so grand."

But if Mabel had no diamonds, she had beauty—and beauty is a magnet that has a way of attracting the heart's desire. Mabel craved diamonds. And so, what do you think?

The careers of Peggy and Mabel ran parallel along the road to wealth, fashion, luxury and husbands. If Peggy had the slight edge on Mabel in the number of marriages, Mabel was one up on Peggy in the diamond department.

Included in her collection was supposed to be a big hunk of the Romanoff crown jewels, reputedly given her by Señor Emil Pardo, ridiculously rich Brazilian coffee planter.

Those jewels, sold by the Soviet, had been contrabanded into the United States by an individual said in hush-hush circles to have been a prince. The royal baubles had a more fantastic and fabulous background than the famous late Mrs. Evelyn Walsh McLean's Hope hoodoo rock.

In 1922, the then Prince of Wales, now Duke of Windsor, visited Canada. Patriotic Canadians thought it would be jolly if he were to take a Canadian girl as a bride. They tapped Lady May Cambridge for the honor. The rumor grew so positive, the match was reported a certainty. A smart Canadian promoter got an inspiration to raise a half-million dollars by public subscription, buy the Romanoff jewels and have them studded into a necklace as a wedding gift for the Queen-to-be.

It all came to naught when the Prince announced he was not engaged to Lady May, had no intention of marrying. But the necklace had been made. It was a miracle of craftsmanship, consisting of 17 beautiful marquise diamonds and one huge egg-shaped clear blue-white diamond pendant that must have weighed 100 carats.

The promoter went broke, couldn't pay off the New York jeweler who executed the piece. The Maiden Lane merchant's bank took the necklace. Then came the depression.

Even banks needed money, so this one turned the gems over to a free-lance broker, who took them to Paris and showed them to La Boll, then the Queen of the Boulevards.

It was love at first blink. And when Pardo asked her what she wanted for Christmas, she already had the answer.

They were a swell investment for her, too. A few years later, when she no longer knew the rich Brazilian and was a little short, she sold the necklace to Harry Winston, the New York jeweler, who recently bought the Jonkers diamond. Winston paid her about $350,-000, cash.

The guy who knows about such things said her collection was worth $3,000,000. Peggy's is valued at only $2,500,000. Poor kid!

Today's GPs don't do nearly so well. Taxes being as they are, they can't expect to.

* * *

Back on the migration of sweet pastry to Manhattan, consider another idiosyncrasy of New York night life.

In other towns—even the largest—the young boys own flivvers or borrow the family car and there are places in the country to drive to. And you can neck on the front porch or in the back yard, or at the barn dance or on a slab in the cemetery.

There's none of those in New York.

Most people live in cramped flats, where even the living room often is used as sleeping quarters.

The young femme can't entertain the young male at home; he usually hasn't a car, and if he had, there's nowhere much to drive to.

Most New York kids court in dark movies, kiss in hallways and doorways, and it's difficult to learn the fine points of love—or even of smooching—in such an environment.

So, in the wisest burg of all, the newcomer is wiser than the native.

18. MODELS

THE HIGHLY paid babes who pose for the photographers are prettier but dumber than their sisters who hoof in the choruses.

Also, they're not as lively.

They may be more photogenic, yet usually they exude about the same amount of personality as those other models—the wax ones in Macy's window.

But they aren't as witless as they act. The average 18-year-old who poses for a living knocks down $100 a week; a good cover (on a mag) type makes as much as $250, and a $500 week is not unknown to the cream of the calling.

Hold your hosses, kids. Don't rush into town. It's just about as difficult to get pacted by one of the three leading agents, John Robert Powers, Harry Conover or Walter Thornton, as it is to wangle a movie contract.

Usually, a model earns more than a so-called contract girl in films, who often signs at $75 a week.

Many models have gone into films as stars. Others have made favorable marriages. (Definition: FAVORABLE—Moolah.)

Some of the town's top party-girls are models. You see them in all the best places, like Morocco and the Stork, with wine-buyers and wolves.

But most models are quiet, unobtrusive kids, who come to New York breathless and bug-eyed.

There are hundreds of them. All day you see them

all over the East Side, scurrying from one advertising agency to another and from one photographer to another.

You usually can spot them, because they invariably carry their make-up and accessories in a Cavanagh, Knox or Dobbs' cardboard hat-box instead of a bag. Those are the insignia of their profession.

They live at the Barbizon for Women, the Shelton, the Beaux Arts, Tudor City and other similar East Side hotels, and they lunch along the counter at 247 Park Avenue and 420 Lexington Avenue, buildings in which models' agents, advertisers and photographers have headquarters.

At cocktail time, you usually find those with dates at Armando's or the Little Club.

Few models flash expensive furs or clothes, yet they are natty and neat, clean-cut, with small features, streamlined, slender and sober.

But these luminous lollipops are responsible for a pernicious influence in dress. Even the most girlish wear girdles, in a mistaken notion it makes their gowns look more slinky.

How really silly! There is nothing cuter than an undulating form swaying to a rumba band. And it's unfair to an escort to clasp a handful of rubber and steel when dancing—instead of something warm and human.

It's really simple, the way the New York girl-grabbers snag the new models.

There's a clique composed of guys who throw cocktail parties, and they manage to keep on excellent terms with the leading models' agents, photographers and publicity boys.

When they hear about a new subject in town, they throw a party in her honor and invite all the others in the gang.

Some are wealthy. But others make a very good living at the thing.

One gimmick is to tax all the male guests a "pro rata" share for the cost of the party, with it generally understood that the host is a major expense.

More indirectly, these connivers, known in other walks by an ugly four-letter word, get by through carrying files of desirable phone numbers.

Some of these characters have "pocket" businesses, such as the sale of diamonds or furs, and every time they complete an introduction to a money-man, the patron is expected to buy a hunk of jewelry or a neck-piece from the go-between, as a gift to the gal.

No classification or occupation is faked as much as that of model.

Many have filed their names with one of the big agents, maybe even done a couple of jobs. But they soon find other means to make money, less arduous than standing on their feet eight hours a day under hot Kleig lights, more steady than awaiting calls for their type.

The term "model" is loosely kicked around in New York and it covers a multitude of skins.

It's difficult for a stranger to meet a real one—that is, unless he has friends in one of the allied businesses, such as advertising, publicity or art.

We are, of course, referring to photographers' models.

There are classifications—much larger—of the ones who model fashions. They should be called mannequins, but that seems a word used only in Paris.

Every wholesale house in the huge cloak and suit industry employs at least one model and all the swank retail stores have whole staffs.

The girls who do this kind of work usually aren't as pretty as the babes who pose for cameras. Facial beauty is not a requisite, although a figure is supposed to be perfect in proportions, to fit commercial dimensions.

Many who work in the wholesale market are friendly and it is considered a regular part of their paid work to "entertain" the big buyer from Burlington.

Many models—photographers' models, that is—go into show business as chorus girls and, conversely, many chorines double as models.

Many of these have the most amazing experiences, and whenever tales like the one about redheaded Joanne Marshall are told, another thousand half-baked pigeons run away from their homes and hotfoot it to New York:

Joanne Marshall, whose real name was Joan Lacock, was born in Wheeling, W. Va., in the summer of 1922.

Her father ran a drugstore. She grew up, the average small-town girl, but shapely, lovely and with the most luminous eyes.

After her father's death, which left the family—her mother and her young brother—about destitute, she and Mrs. Lacock came to New York. Joanne was so entrancingly beautiful, she had little trouble catching on as a model, and quickly earned $75 to $100 a week. She was then about 18.

Some of the other Powers exhibits told her about the offer they had to become show girls in the new revue being prepared to star Al Jolson.

It would be loads of fun. Joanne joined the show, too.

It opened in Chicago in the summer of 1940, then made its Gotham debut that fall. Joanne was crazy about it.

Until then, she knew no serious romances.

Her male companions were young men without serious intentions; youths like Gar Wood, Jr., and George Church, a young dancer in the show, and George Miller, an equally young chorus boy.

One day the great man who starred in the show, the fabulous Jolson, tiffed with Jinx Falkenberg, then a featured show gal in the production, since then a film starlet and "breakfast broadcaster."

Jinx had often gone out with Al after his break-up with Ruby Keeler.

Jolson turned away, suddenly noticed the 18-year-old child who had been dancing, unseen by him, in his own chorus.

He took the gal to dinner, flattered her beyond anything she had heard in West Virginia or from youthful New Yorkers.

He swept her practically off her feet.

We say "practically," advisedly.

For, though she gave the air to all the boys, much to

their anguish and unflattering cracks about the age of her new friend, she resisted Jolson's importuning to marry her.

Yet she was seen with him nightly, shared his favorite corner table at the Stork Club after every show, took him home to meet her family, did not deny published reports that this was the real thing.

The wise Willies said, "See what happens when an old guy with fame and dough comes along? He gets the rail post." So they thought.

They didn't even know about a good-looking young fellow who sang with a band.

Joanne met him in a night club, dated him one night when Jolson was busy elsewhere. He began to take up more and more of her time. Then she married him. It was at about the time he began to click on the radio. He did okay. He is now a top Hollywood star. His name is Dick Haymes. And Joanne is now Joan Dru, married to her second husband, actor John Ireland.

Earlier in this chapter, we implied that models are dumb. Most of them are. But one who was no dope was a blue-eyed rusty-mop who graduated from the local high school in Canton, N.C., at 13. Dumb, did we say? High school is correct. She finished it at 13.

Her name was Marianne Grey.

The next year, she matriculated at the University of Wisconsin, its youngest student. She majored in archeology—bone-dry digging up of things long dead. She got her degree in three years, at 17.

Luckily, all her spadework couldn't retard her physical development. She had curves and dimples wherever bewitching beauts at 17 can grow curves and dimples.

Carefully packing her sheepskin in mothballs, Marianne, the tomb-expert, set out to rummage around in the living world. She found it strangely clammy to specialists on mummies.

It might, though, find itself short of curves and dimples, red hair and blue eyes.

So Marianne Grey changed her diploma-distinguished name to Marianne Simms and headed for Broadway, where she registered it on the rolls of Powers' models.

All students of the Sunday supplements know these dolls get around and everybody looks at them.

In her peregrinations, she met Sinclair Lewis, who, captivated more by her ravishments than by her knowledge of King Tut, brought her to the attention of Edna and Red Skelton. They signed her to a personal contract pronto, brought her to Hollywood for a projected radio show—Skeltons instead of skeletons.

The show didn't materialize. But David O. Selznick did.

The great producer offered a screen test. Literate as well as gorgeous, the youngster wrote the script of the test, and in it she challenged the camera.

When she signed the contract, her name was changed again—to Cristofa Sims and she became a Hollywood favorite.

WISDOM OF A WHITE WAY WOLF:

Smart guys seldom escort Powers, Thornton or Conover models. The cover gals arise so early to keep working appointments that, along about midnight, as the party gets in high, they suggest you take them home. Chorines and show gals are indicated for night owls. Models are for chumps who crave to show off with orchidaceous bric-a-brac.

19. SECOND FROM THE END

SO MANY millions of inspirational and incoherent words are annually written in raves over New York's chorus gals that the time has come to do a little debunking.

1. Our chorines are not the prettiest girls in the world.
2. Nor are they the most immoral—
3. Or the most stupid.
4. They are usually poor dressers.
5. Few have passable gowns.
6. A small number live in penthouses.
7. Fewer win rich patrons or sweeties.

The New York rolls of Chorus Equity and the American Guild of Variety Artists list several thousand girls who work in the ensembles of musical shows, vaudeville houses and night clubs, or road-show in traveling theatrical troupes, tabloid units, circuses and carnivals originating in New York.

Of these, not more than ten tyros in any year come forth as glamor gals, and the proportion of those with outstanding beauty is just about the same as in non-professional life.

New York's chorines, like her models, are drawn to the magnet from every state in the Union and all corners of the earth. Few hit the jackpot.

Many Hollywood femme stars once hoofed in Broadway lines and other cuties snared rich husbands or near-husbands.

But for every Paulette Goddard, Barbara Stanwyck, Alice Faye, Joan Crawford and Lucille Bremer, there are thousands of kids who pound out the soles of their aching feet for five or six years, then discover that at 21 or 22 they've been around the Stem so long the managers call them "old faces" and they no longer can get work.

If they have no particular talent to develop into individual specialties, or if they haven't the faculty to snare a man to take care of them, they've got to get jobs in inferior outlying night clubs or in out-of-town cafés or road-shows, and, typed as a "road louse," there is only one direction for them—down.

Yet nothing deters recruits. For every one who gets a Broadway job, there are 100 applicants.

Perhaps, because we're getting older, we mumble that "those days" were the best.

But the records prove the current chorus gal is not half so gay, glamorous or interesting as the ensemble entry of a decade and more ago.

The world has changed, and with it changed the choryphee.

In the old days, a chorus salary of 50 or 60 bucks a week seemed like a million to hicks in the sticks, and parental opposition was not too oppressive.

The playboys were still around; the mobsters rustled $1,000 bills and the Wall Street Blue Sky subdividers had gold mines up there.

Now, a survey will turn up the startling fact that most lilies of the line are using the chorus as a temporary makeshift while completing their education. They double between the cabaret floor or stage, and college. If they're seeking a theatrical career, they spend their days studying voice, ballet, dramatics.

The result is, few playgirls at that source. More and more duck home immediately after the show, so they can get up early and go to school or to the coach.

This is very bad on love-life, and the few still around with loose shekels don't look too longingly at Broadway.

It's getting extremely difficult to meet a chorus charmer.

Those in legit musicals aren't usually approachable unless you know someone to perform the introductions, which makes this puzzle something like the one about which came first, the egg or the chicken.

Night club quail is as hard to make up to, because of the law which forbids entertainers to sit with patrons in the dining room. All big cafés, with the choicest, enforce this rule rigorously. You'd hardly want to meet the girls in the kind of dumps that cheat.

Thus, the new babe has little opportunity to get in with the playboy set. There are, of course, exceptions. People still break out of Leavenworth, too.

The glamorous ten who crack through each year, to be quoted and itemed in the columns, wined and steaked at El Morocco and screen-tested by 20th Century-Fox are the phenoms.

The others go home every night and study—or end up with a musician.

That's orthodox.

Every night club and theatre with choruses must employ musicians. They work the same bastard hours as the girls. They duck out for smokes at the same time, have their crullers and java in the same lunchroom or greasy spoon. They talk the same language about the same interests.

Propinquity, plus opportunity, are Cupid's nets.

The young, strange gals are lonesome, their cheap rooms are depressing—and musicians are at their elbows.

So you can easily figure out the answer to this one: To meet a chorine, learn to slide a trombone.

Most of the kids live in midtown hotels between Sixth and Eighth Avenues, from 42nd Street to 55th.

Their favorites are the Piccadilly, Forrest, President, Plymouth, Belvedere, Victoria, Taft, Abbey, Century, Knickerbocker, Wellington, with those who can afford it staying at the Edison, Lincoln, Astor and Park Sheraton and dreaming of the Savoy Plaza.

A day in the life of the average chorine—without school obligations—would find her arising about 5 P.M., and getting out just in time to grab a cup of coffee before reporting for work. They look like hell at this time of day, minus make-up and with tousled hair in a net. The transformation that comes after they apply their stage war paint remains with them for the rest of the day. When a chorine has a date after or between shows, she never removes the pancake or the drugstore eyelashes.

When they are eating alone or with a musician boy friend (with whom they usually go "Dutch") you'll find them at the soda fountains of Hanson's pharmacy, 51st and Seventh Avenue, or the Paramount druggist, on Seventh near 52nd Street. Their favorite lunch counters are Rudley's and Rikers, and the greasy vest in the 49th Street side of the Brill Building.

Those who aren't cabaret hoppers frequently bowl at the Roxy alley after the show. Others prefer jam sessions in the small and smoky 52nd Street jitterbug joints.

* * *

The ambition of every cookie in every chorus is to be tapped by a Hollywood talent scout.

Each year several dozen "new faces" are approached by the local representatives of the major film studios and signed to "option contracts," with the company not obligated to hire the girl after she is tested.

A tiny percentage of those so signed arrive in Hollywood, and of these one in a thousand makes good.

Often they seek out your authors and breathlessly spill the info that it has come—the chance for a screen test!

What to do?

We ask whether the test is to be shot here or on the Coast. Mostly likely, it's in the New York studios.

We caution, "Don't take it; hold out for a Coast test."

173

Few movie contracts have resulted from tests in local offices here. The facilities and abilities available are undergrade. The best points are not brought out. There are no directors here, so any talent that does lurk is often kicked around.

But when a studio has enough faith to ship one to the Coast for the test, chances of a film break-through are considerably higher.

First, the studio must pay a salary during the testing period, on top of round-trip, first-class fare. With that invested, efforts will be made to bring out assets. And, should the first test fizzle, others will be given.

Another factor against Eastern tests is that the try-out is viewed by a tough jury, 3,000 miles away—hard strangers predisposed to turn thick thumbs down.

In addition to meaning little, these Eastern screen tests are a walkaway for wise wolves, most of whom manage to get close to casting agents of studios.

The procedure is to introduce the subject to the scout and get his promise to consider her for a test. Even if he eventually turns her down, the squab is on a string for weeks and has to be nice to her "benefactor." If she ever gets the test, she's hooked for at least three months, while the film is shipped to the Coast to await the verdict of producers and directors.

Actually, it's not necessary to know anyone to get consideration from the talent scouts. They're always looking for new faces. That's their business. Just barge in. (See page 301 for list of casting agents.)

But, suppose the candidate is lucky enough to run the gauntlet and find herself signed to the usual standard contract, which calls for $125 per week the first six months and options for seven years thereafter, at a slowly rising scale.

Should she take it?

We say, unless she wants the trip and a six-month paid vacation—no. She wants to be a dramatic actress. The odds against her making any talking screen role are about one in 500. If her heart breaks easily, movies will do it.

We tell her when she steps off the Super-Chief, with high hopes and enthusiasm, she will be plugged, for publicity, as a new star. A battery of photogs will greet her at Union Station. That afternoon she will get phone calls from every chaser in town, who will have learned everything about her by the grapevine from their opposite numbers in New York, who kissed her good-bye.

The first week will be a merry-go-round. She will dance till she's dippy at the Sunset Strip cabarets, meeting the biggies and the host of peculiar paranoiacs who infest the colony. She will go to swimming pool parties at mansions that look like De Mille film sets.

But the cabarets are fewer and not so glamorous as those she left behind. The people are duller, less intriguing. After a week, she'll realize Hollywood is pretty much Petoskey with palms.

Then will come the waiting—waiting for calls from the studio, waiting for appointments with the costumers, hairdressers, publicity department, still photogs.

She'll be snapped in every pose. If she's ultra-photogenic, she's sunk. For the rest of her career in Hollywood, while her gams are still straight and her figure otherwise, she'll pose cheese-cake for fan-mags and Sunday sheets—and find herself with a one-way ticket back to New York six months later.

The girl, of the hundreds under contract at every lot, who gets the attention of the producer or director, so he throws her a line in a picture, is the lucky one who is hit by a modern miracle.

She is the one each year at each studio who may possibly have a future.

The others, perhaps equally qualified, return to New York and sarcastic jibes, go back to the farm and marry the hired hand, or remain a part of the Hollywood flotsam, drifting from one extra call to another, back to a job in a chorus, possibly end up as a car-hop or checkroom-worker, as many have and will.

But, as we hinted, in New York dreams sometimes do come alive, though not always according to time-table or preconceived plan.

In the spring of 1937, Mortimer received a phone call from a 15-year-old redhead named Marianne O'Brien, who that day had joined the kid chorus of Ben Marden's Riviera, a glittering roadhouse on the New Jersey side of the George Washington Bridge.

Said Miss O'Brien to Mortimer: "I'm 15, sweet, unspoiled and innocent. Rich men like to marry girls like me, the others tell me. Will you take me to the Stork Club and introduce me to one?"

Mortimer is an obliging soul, especially when he smells a story, so he scorted the youngster to Chez Billingsley, but ran into no millionaires.

Marianne got no proposals of marriage that season, but did achieve some attention due to publication of the following story:

It seems Ben Marden demanded all "new faces" for his chorus that year. When he interviewed Marianne in the line-up, he said, "Wait a minute, dear, haven't you worked for me before?"

Marianne demurely replied, "No, sir, you mistake me for my mamma, Mae O'Brien, who danced in your chorus at the Silver Slipper a few years ago."

Mae O'Brien, still beautiful and redheaded, was then selling programs and cigarettes at Jimmy Kelly's Greenwich Village bistro.

Marianne missed out on her millionaire, but soon the public prints linked her with many other men. She was pursued like the rabbit in a greyhound race. She was in demand as a photographers' model and finally won a speaking role in a road show of a Broadway hit.

A talent scout from Warners saw her, signed her to a $750 a week contract. She sat in Hollywood a year, on the payroll but not on a work-sheet. She was credited with romances in dizzy dozens, yet none with millionaires.

Then her film "career" faded and Marianne returned to New York. They said she was "through," though she was 22.

In the meantime, her mother, Mae, a widow, had wed. Her husband was no millionaire, but he got by. His name is Abe Attell, and three decades ago he was the world's featherweight champion, called by many the greatest boxer ever.

He had achieved fame of another sort by being named as the go-between in the Black Sox baseball scandal.

One night at El Morocco, Marianne was introduced to a good-looking, youngish fellow, who wanted to dance with her. He asked for a date. It grew into a romance.

The man, Richard Reynolds, Jr., heir to the $30,-000,000 tobacco fortune, settled with his wife for $3,000,000—to be free to marry Marianne.

So the little redhead, no longer 15 or so unsophisticated, got her millionaire. No wonder O. Henry, who wrote so much so well about a town he knew so little, called it Bagdad on the Subway. It's a wonderworld— to its chosen few.

20. PARTY GIRLS

JUST WHAT and who is the party girl? Where does she come from? How does she live? What does she make?

There is a great deal of popular misinformation about the "party girl" and her function. The common error is to confuse her with a "call girl" and let it go at that. But there is a great and definite distinction between the two, though, of course, there are borderline cases.

But which is the "party girl"? You'll find her in many East Side hotels and apartment houses. Originally, she came to New York or Hollywood from Texas, Oklahoma, Florida or a small Pennsylvania town, with ambitions to become a model or an actress.

More often than not, her name is registered at one or more of the large model agencies.

All new girls in town quickly find themselves invited to cocktail parties given in swank apartments, where the local wolves get an opportunity to look them over.

These parties usually are thrown by hosts who make their living that way. They are smooth, suave characters with an unlimited acquaintance among show people, artists and models, and have access to every fresh young thing in town.

In return, the "guests" pay liberally for the privilege of being invited to the parties and also reward their hosts liberally otherwise, such as buying fur coats or jewelry through them, giving them tips on the market or commissions on deals consummated through contacts made at these parties.

The new girl in town soon finds she can make a good living merely by gracing these parties, and at the same time have a lot of fun with practically no labor or exertion. The usual fee these days is from $50 up, and the "party girl" is, unlike the "call girl," under no obligation whatever to give more than her presence.

What she does on her own, of course, is her own business. But many are good businesswomen. Quite often a "party girl" ends up with a wealthy protector and a luxurious apartment, if not marriage.

Many "party girls" have no means of support other than their fees for being on call to go out dancing. Some, however, continue to work as chorines or models, thus enhancing their desirability as guests and taking down the wages of toil. The girl with ambition to go places in show business often finds being a "party girl" a stepping stone toward a contract.

Many of the clients are visiting film executives who are lonesome and want to go out with a pretty girl, a semi-professional preferred, jailbait and film personnel avoided with horror.

The chief qualifications of a successful "party girl" are good looks, a range of smart clothes with the know-how to wear them, some wit, a fund of the day's small talk, superior dancing ability and a sense of humor—and, above almost all, she must be a good listener. She probably hears more bragging than she does "propositioning."

Clients fall into a variety of classifications. There are big businessmen with heavy deals to close, who find pretty girls help break down a customer's resistance. There are wealthy men who occasionally want to go out for a night on the town with a charming companion and no complications. And there are, of course, plain wolves.

"Party girls," unlike "call girls," are welcomed in all the best places in town and travel in the top strata of society—or, at least, café society. As steerers to some clubs they get commissions. All headwaiters know them, but none recognizes them.

21. IT COULD ONLY HAPPEN ON BROADWAY

*T*HE CHARACTERS O. Henry, Damon Runyon, and Mark Hellinger wrote about were fictitious. None like them ever existed in New York or elsewhere. They were broad inventions that lived only in their gifted creators' imaginations.

Here are some Broadway beauts who actually lived and did make history. These stories are not fiction:

a.—*The Carrot Top and the Opal*

Iris Adrian, an oomphy redhead, who now plays tough girl parts in films, was a central character in one of the strangest love stories ever told on Broadway.

She had come to New York a young greenhorn, in 1932, from her California home.

She had no ambitions toward show business, but was visiting a girl friend, who one day answered a call posted by the late great Flo Ziegfeld. Iris went along to watch.

Ziegfeld didn't hire the friend, but he asked Iris if she would like to be a glorified clothes-horse. Iris thought it might be a lark and took the job.

At that time N.T.G., who was running the old Hollywood Restaurant on Broadway, had an agreement with Ziegfeld that the ten choicest Ziegfeld girls could double in both shows. Iris was one of the ten, easy.

Every night, after the final curtain of the Ziegfeld show—it was *Hot-Cha,* in which the late tempestuous Lupe Velez starred—Iris would scamper to the Hollywood and go into the chorus there for the midnight and two o'clock performances.

One of the owners of the Hollywood Restaurant was a very wealthy New York real estate man. His son, Herman Amron, was manager of the club. He fell in love with Iris and for a year or more it was one of the torrid romances of the Street.

When Iris took a summer off to go to Europe, Herman grabbed the next boat and followed her. When she returned, he bought her a mink coat, a diamond ring, a diamond bracelet—and kept buying.

He loved her so much, he did what so many other unwise, over-eager men on Broadway do. He tried to help her career. He begged talent scouts to go to see Iris. He spoke to friends—in the movie studios. Finally Iris came up with a contract—a year, with options each six months. She went out to Hollywood about ten years ago and appeared first in a George Raft picture. Herman was thrilled that he had done so much for his beloved. But, of course, he was very lonesome, since his job kept him here. He managed to fly out a couple of times to see her, but, as so many other men have learned, he found fame and adulation help a girl forget the man who isn't there.

Herman felt he was losing her. He grew desperate. He was back in New York. Christmas was coming. He had bought her diamonds and furs and didn't know what to send her now. He chose a beautiful, costly opal bracelet, packed it carefully, put in an affectionate card and sent it on to Hollywood, to Iris.

What Herman didn't know was, that among the superstitions in show business—like not whistling in a dressing-room or wearing yellow on opening night—opals are hoodoo 1-A.

Iris received the package. Like a girl, she opened it in a flurry of anticipation. She took out the opal bracelet. It was beautiful and she put it on, though she knew it was hard luck.

In the same mail was a letter from her studio—a notice that her option wasn't taken up and in two weeks she would no longer shine at Paramount.

The two, coming at once, were more than a coincidence to Iris. She knew that the opals had jinxed her contract. In a rage, she threw the bracelet on the floor, broke a couple of stones, had her maid send it back.

Two days later, still furious, she married a man who had been proposing to her for a year. He was worth $30,000,000, but he had one drawback—he was deaf and dumb.

The honeymoon covered a cruise from California to New York, via the Panama Canal. When Iris got to New York, she left him, picked a good state and sued for divorce. She got her decree and, washed up with pictures, returned to New York clubs, this time doing a specialty, advertised as Iris Adrian of the films.

She worked a couple of weeks at Leon & Eddie's, featured, and got over so well that she was given another chance in Hollywood, with another studio. And this time she clicked.

Through the years, Herman Amron continued to love her. Once in a while she would give him a break and let him take her out. Though he had disposed of the opal bracelet years before, the curse apparently hung on. Every time she went out with Herman something unfortunate happened to her.

Once she got sick; again, she got word of a lost Hollywood contract.

The last time Iris was in the newspapers was when she married Georgie Jay, a personable character who owns an uptown night club, the 78th Street Taproom. The marriage, of course, wasn't meant to take, because Iris had to stay in Hollywood and he had to stay in New York.

Once, when she was East, she and her husband sat in Leon & Eddie's. Herman, the hoodoo, was at the next table. He came over to say hello to Iris and Jay. That night Iris and her husband had the squabble which resulted, a week later, in her divorce.

b.—*Edith Finds Love*

Newcomers to night life—and most people around town today—will not recognize her name, Edith Roark.

But we remember Edith well—also the fabulously funny story she told on herself, that made her for the time the best-known beauty on the White Way.

Edith came from Dallas . . . went to Hollywood . . . became a showgirl . . . worked for Sam Goldwyn.

When N.T.G. opened the famous old Paradise Restaurant on Broadway, in 1932, he imported 12 Goldwyn girls—at $150 a week—for his première. Edith was one.

On the Coast, the luminous Miss Roark had been the constant companion of George Raft.

In New York, she met singer Harry Richman—my, how that guy gets into our stories!—and became his constant companion.

A few months later, Richman and Raft happened to meet in Chicago.

Raft said to Richman—"Harry, what's this I hear about you trying to steal my girl?"

Richman said to Raft—"Georgie, you're nuts. She's my girl and you keep away from her."

Raft replied—"I'll prove it."

He phoned Edith in New York, said—"Honey, Richman says you love him."

Miss Roark, not knowing Richman was listening in on the extension, cooed sweetly—"Why, Georgie, you know you're my only love. I'm just being polite to Richman. He's important and can do me good."

"Just wait till I call her," Richman said.

He got Edith on the phone, asked—"What's this I hear about Raft?"

Again cooing sweetly, unconscious of Raft's ear on the other receiver, Edith said—"Why, Harry, you know you're my only love. I'm just being polite to Raft. He was so nice to me on the Coast."

The pay-off is that when the two stars accused her of double dealing, Edith flew into a simulated rage, shouted she knew they were testing her all the time and she said it all on purpose.

She made them both apologize to her—in the presence of her real sweetheart!

c.—*Unto the Second Generation*

It's likely you have heard of Hilda Ferguson, even possible you vaguely remember her. But it is not likely you have heard of Yolande Ugarte, who did do a bit in a Broadway show which ran about a week.

This is the story to date of Yolande Ugarte, and so it must also be to a degree the story of Hilda Ferguson, because Yolande, now in her 20's, seemed compelled by a strange destiny to follow in the footsteps of her mother, Hilda Ferguson.

During the first 17 years of her life, Yolande led a sheltered existence with relatives in Baltimore. She went to school, had puppy-love crushes. And, like many girls of her age, she dreamed of the stage.

She had a vague notion that her mother, whom she hadn't seen for years, had something to do with Broadway. Beyond that she knew little about her. The mother's name was seldom mentioned where she lived.

One summer Yolande entered a beauty contest. She was chosen to represent Baltimore in the annual Atlantic City competitions. Her guardians hated to see her go, but her youthful, understandable enthusiasm overcame all objections.

Many Broadway producers visited the resort town the week "Miss America" was chosen. Among those seeking new faces for shows were Earl Carroll and Nils T. Granlund.

Yolande Ugarte is an attractive girl: tall, lissome, with nut-brown hair. The producers were much taken with her possibilities. They thought there was something vaguely reminiscent of Hilda Ferguson about Yolande. Granlund, who had been Hilda's press agent 15 years before, told her so.

"Hilda Ferguson? Why, I believe my mother used that name," Yolande replied.

He hired Yolande as a dancer in his new cabaret, the Midnight Sun. He changed her name to "Hilda Ferguson." She was startlingly like her mother and Broadway was thrilled when Granlund introduced her as "Hilda Ferguson."

The original Hilda Ferguson was a dainty, devastating beauty, born in Baltimore as Hilda Gibbons. At 15, she eloped with and married a young Honduran medical student, Ramond Ugarte. Yolande was born the next year.

Hilda and her husband separated soon afterward. Hilda came to New York and baby Yolande was left with relatives, with whom she lived thenceforth.

They still tell stories about the wide-eyed Hilda Ferguson, strange in New York, only 17, still naïve, though a grass widow and a mother.

It took her little time to make the grade. She became a "Follies" girl. Ziegfeld featured her as one of his most beautiful. Then started the hectic career that to Broadwayites made the name "Hilda Ferguson" symbolize an era. Hilda came to Broadway in 1921, shortly after the beginning of Prohibition. Churchill's, Rectors, Reisenweber's, Bustanoby's, the Café de Paris, were fresh, green memories.

The speakeasies were getting going. The first of the bootleggers, later to inspire a bloody generation of crime, were feeling their way in wholesale law violation.

In this changing world, the girl decided to cast her lot.

Her tinseled career, running a parallel course with Prohibition, came to an end on a hospital cot two months and two days before Repeal.

During her short lifetime, Hilda went the pace with men and liquor. Young millionaires and old ones, powerful figures of the underworld and of politics were on the roster of her admirers. Her life reads like a history of America's crazy years.

She was a flat-mate of Dot King when the mysterious slaying of that youngster, kept by a Philadelphia financier, rocked Manhattan.

Hilda, questioned by police, denied she knew a thing about it.

She was engaged to Aaron Benesch, multi-millionaire Baltimore furniture king, only to lose him to Helen Henderson, another glamorous show girl.

She was the sweetheart of Enoch (Nucky) Johnson, Atlantic City overlord, and was featured by him in an elaborate show in Atlantic City's Silver Slipper, a night club he bought for the sole purpose of providing a stage for his current reigning favorite.

He gave her a $12,000 mink coat and a Rolls-Royce. They lived in half the second floor of the Ritz-Carlton.

She lost him to Kitty Ray, who claimed she was the ex-wife of Macoco, millionaire playboy of the Pampas, though he denied they ever wed.

Arthur Hammerstein was one of her most ardent admirers. Then it was rumored Hilda would marry Howard Lee, rich society scion.

She was questioned by police when "Tough Willie" McCabe, ex-bodyguard of Arnold Rothstein, was cut up in the "61 Club" stabbings. To General Sessions Judge Freschi, she exclaimed: "My dear, I was in the ladies' room."

The judge replied: "It's very nice to be called 'my dear.' I don't know whether I like it or not."

He held her in $5,000 bail. She spent the night in Harlem Prison until she was bailed out the next day by "Feets" Edson, another colorful Broadway mobster.

"I put up the bail," Edson said, "because she used to work for me." Hilda had appeared in the Club Abbey, another resort of pungent Broadway memory, where Larry Fay was later killed.

She had refused to talk after Dot King was slain. She kept mum when police grilled her about Willie McCabe. Broadway said: "Hilda knows how to keep her mouth shut."

So she forfeited the $5,000 bail for failing to appear.

When third-degreed about her dressing-room mate in *The Music Box Revue*—who was thought to have landed her job because her father was warden of Leavenworth Prison, where Nicky Arnstein, husband of Fannie Brice, star of the show, was on the rock pile— Hilda again "knew nothing."

She started her own little brownstone-front upstairs speakeasy. The opening was all New York in one place. It was soon the scene of raids and battles.

When she went to Europe to duck a judgment she resented, for $270 for ten pairs of specially built shoes, she traveled incognito, with her Rolls-Royce, two maids and 27 trunks.

Though she never earned more than $150 a week, Hilda once walked into Texas Guinan's, and bought a bracelet off Tex's arm for $25,000 in big bills, just to "burn up" Kitty Ray, who was sitting a few tables away with "Nucky" Johnson.

She was 29 when she died, in New York Hospital, of peritonitis.

Many of her friends are still on Broadway. At least one gentleman with whom she was known to be close cracked a bottle of champagne for her daughter.

A girl who also succeeded Hilda in the affections of "Nucky" Johnson worked at the same club with her daughter until she left to get married. With a subtle touch of irony, fate had decreed that this girl, Virginia Biddle, should dance next to Yolande Ugarte, Hilda Ferguson's daughter!

Hilda, Junior, after sweeping Broadway's most ardent off their feet, eloped with Frank Parker, radio tenor. The marriage, a stormy one, lasted all of two years, after which the pair took their troubles to court.

The court decision which severed their ties only brought more squabbles in its wake. For, when Hilda, Junior, became the constant companion of Duncan Mc-Martin, Canadian multimillionaire, and McMartin's wife inferred she was the cause of their separation, Parker hailed Hilda back into court.

He told the judge she was holding him up to so much ridicule he thought alimony payments should be stopped. The judge said Frank was no candidate for a monastery either, and ordered the payments to go on, with an urgent reminder to get the arrears up to date.

As these lines were written McMartin settled with his wife, obtained a divorce and married Hilda.

d.—*The Good Deed*

When Ruth Hilliard was eight years old, she was scalded by boiling water. One side of her face was terribly disfigured. When she grew up, she would have been beautiful enough, except for that hideous scar.

She worked as a cigarette girl in the old Hollywood Restaurant, and envied the chorines who had all the nice things in life.

Stars thronged the Hollywood, and so did the millionaires. But none noticed Ruth Hilliard. Or, if they did, it was to look at the scar and momentarily think, "what a shame!"

A constant visitor at the Hollywood was Jimmy Ritz, the comedian. Ruth often wished he'd say hello to her. Sometimes, when she had the money, she'd go to Loew's State to see him act, or to Earl Carroll's *Vanities*, in which he later starred.

One night, William Leeds, Jr., fabulously rich son of the Tin Plate King, bought a cigar from Ruth. He saw the scar, asked about it, took down her name and address. The next day Ruth's mother got a phone call from Leeds. He said he had made arrangements with a plastic surgeon to operate on her; had paid all the bills in advance. It seemed unbelievable, but Ruth and her mother visited the medico, the operation was decided on and Ruth went into a hospital.

Meanwhile, Leeds sailed away on a year's yachting cruise.

On his return, he and his fiancée, Olive Hamilton, later Mrs. Leeds, went to the *Vanities*.

A girl in the front line seemed familiar. After the show, the girl ran over to Leeds, threw her arms around him, showered him with blessings. She was Ruth Hilliard. The operation had been a complete success. But Leeds had forgotten all about his impulsive gracious gesture.

Ruth Hilliard had sighed and prayed to be like other girls, so that maybe Jimmy Ritz would notice her and take her out. He and his brothers were stars of the show in which she hoofed—and, sure enough, he did notice her. He took her out. A romance developed.

They were engaged a long time, then married.

Everyone figured Ruth now would be happy forever after. From an ugly duckling she had become a beautiful show girl. She got the man she always wanted. She went to Hollywood when the Ritzes were at the height of their fame and lived lavishly. She got a movie contract, too.

Though she later divorced Ritz, she remarried and is now living in Hollywood, happy and prosperous.

It's another of those things that could only happen on Broadway.

And it all started because Bill Leeds, Jr., was in a generous mood that night, and played Aladdin's genie to a sad, frustrated girl.

e.—*Gun Moll*

Those were some of the little pigs who went to market and who had roast beef. (And "pigs" is the backstage slang for chorines.) Here's a little round-up on one who had none, and cried "wee-wee-wee" all the way home.

Marion Paterka was born in Boston, in 1908, child of Czech immigrants. Her mother married again, a man named Strasmick, and, as Marion Strasmick, a black-eyed, beautiful redhead, 16, descended on Broadway. You never saw a prettier girl. Ziegfeld never did, as he said when he glorified her on sight for his *Follies*.

In that show there was an ensemble number in which the kids did take-offs on the stars of the day. Lenore Ulric was in Belasco's *Kiki*. Marion impersonated her. She was Kiki the rest of her life. Kiki Roberts she chose to make it. And that name was to shout from Page 1 headlines often—for Kiki became the sweetheart of Jack "Legs" Diamond, gangster, mass killer, riddled so often with bullets that he was dubbed "the clay pigeon of the underworld."

Diamond first saw her in "practice clothes," sweater and bloomers, trying out on a chorus call for *Strike Me Pink,* a revue angeled by gangster dough and starring

Jimmy Durante and Lupe Velez. A dozen or more of "the boys" kittied the bank roll. That gave them the privilege of sitting in. Also of putting their young molls in the line.

As one went through her paces, a partner in the enterprise asked:

"Whose bim is dat one?"

"Nobody's," was the answer.

"Den what's she doin' in our show?"

Diamond took another look and almost fell out of his chair.

"She's mine!" he barked.

And, though she didn't know it yet, she was—so quickly and so suddenly that she didn't even open in the show. Diamond wouldn't let her out of bed long enough even to rehearse.

Not a bad-looking beast, Legs; he got his nickname when he was a boy thief, because he could outrun the bulls. Tall, slender, with regular features, dark and personable, Legs was a night club hound, even owned and ran some himself. He was boss of the Hotsy Totsy. There, one night, cockeyed, he shot two inoffensive customers. There were present, besides the corpses and the well-dressed man with the automatic, seven other men, including Diamond's bartender.

When the cops arrived, Legs had legged it. Within six weeks, those seven—including the bartender—were shot down and killed, one by one. The night of the day the last one cashed in, Legs walked into a police station and asked, charmingly, "You boys looking for me?"

There were no witnesses.

That was the assassin Kiki idolized.

When he was sprayed with lead in the Monticello Hotel, a hide-out for his sort, she was with him. Almost every time, and that time, she was hauled in and put on the carpet. Yes, she was around—but she was asleep—she didn't know from nothing.

Diamond had a younger brother, Eddie, a lunger, his lieutenant. The kid went to Denver for his health. Some New York murderers who hadn't dared molest him while Legs was around followed him and sniped at him. The youngster scrammed back. Legs loved him and when he heard what had happened he boiled, got oiled and went out with two pants-pocket miniature .38's to pay off.

In the next three days, four bodies were found, widely scattered. A meeting was called, a death sentence was passed on Legs Diamond, who had cheated so many such with only some scars as mementos.

Diamond was tipped off. He took it on the lam. He found a secluded cottage up in Sullivan County, a region of apple orchards. But he was a gangster in his heart.

Kiki, again, was with him. She begged him to stay under cover. He had enough money for existence. But Legs had a trade and he went to work.

Applejack had a ready and lucrative market. Diamond started to "organize" the farmers, to buy up their crops. Some yielded, for he offered cash. Others had commitments and refused. They found a muzzle in their bellies and a threat—sell him their apples or else.

196

One, Grover Parks, a young farmer, was game. When Diamond came back he had a pitchfork. But Legs had a cannon. He backed Parks into his barn, strung him up by the wrists and burned the soles of his feet. Parks didn't die. He lived to get the local law to hunt down the stranger in the county. Legs was indicted. Kiki was taken in, too, released on $2,500 bail, cleared. She went back to New York and into another show.

In December, 1931, Diamond was tried, in Troy. He had a brilliant lawyer, Daniel Pryor. After a bitter contest, he was acquitted.

Diamond, all this time, had a wife, Alice. She knew a lot about Kiki—anyone who could read did. But she stuck—when he'd let her.

Kiki was then sharing an apartment with Agnes O'Laughlin, another Ziegfelder (she later made some sensational inconclusive accusations against Rudy Vallee, and, disgusted with the whole life, returned to her native Cleveland and married a boy she'd gone to school with). Kiki was ordered to stay far from Troy. Because of the notoriety with Kiki, Pryor had ordered that Alice Diamond, Legs' wife, sit beside him through the trial.

But there were telephones.

The jury freed Legs about midday. He, Alice, Eddie and Pryor drove to Albany, a few miles off, and staged a celebration dinner. Diamond had engaged a shabby room where he was to spend the night with Alice.

At about 9 o'clock, half overboard, Legs said he was going to the washroom. Instead, he slipped outside, hailed a taxi and was driven to another bed-house, where he had parked Kiki.

At 3 A.M., a very drunken man staggered out and gave the address of the place where Legs had hired sleeping quarters for "J. H. Desmond and Wife," to a hackman. He was unconscious on arrival. The driver pulled him together enough to get him upstairs. Diamond fell into bed with all his clothes on, including his derby hat.

A long, gray limousine had followed him. Five minutes later, it was roaring toward New York. In the bed lay the clay pigeon—this time shot for keeps. Alice and the party were still at the restaurant, waiting for him.

Kiki was questioned. Maybe she had an idea of who her man's enemies had been. Maybe not. She wasn't held.

She went back to Boston. Said she was licked—through. She posed for pictures with her mother, ironing, cooking. But she wasn't through. They never are while they can help it.

She came back, danced in cafés, did fan numbers, worked in Jersey, Pennsylvania, sneaked to New York and was hired at an uptown smalltime spot, the Little Casino. The flatfeet tore down the billing and wouldn't let her work. They said she was a peeler. But it is a policy of New York police not to permit exploitation of names connected with crime stories.

Alice also went into show business, got herself an act in which she preached against liquor, violence and violation of the marriage oath. The dicks gave her the bum's rush, too. Soon thereafter she was put on the spot and murdered. The wise crowd said, "She knew too much."

Kiki drifted. She was reported married to an athletic director, but that fizzled. She did marry a beer salesman, in an elopement, and she soon got a divorce. She flew to Memphis and became the wife of a Newark airport attaché.

She was reported running a lunchroom in Bridgeport. Broadway never knew her again.

Perhaps, somewhere, now 40 but undoubtedly still chic and attractive, a redheaded woman lives the simple, unrippled existence of a matured matron. Perhaps, though, in the dark, alone, she recalls the flash of guns, the thud of bullets, the mad love of a murderous madman, third degrees by police and prosecutors, days and nights of fleeing and being hunted with her lover—and the last glimpse of his riddled remains, in a basket in an undertaker's morgue in Albany, where she slunk in after all others—except one of your authors, covering the story—had gone.

This little pig had no roast beef. But she certainly didn't stay home!

22. WHITE WAY WOLVES

CALL A MAN a dog and he'll fight. Call a woman a cat and she'll scratch your eyes.

But speak of a guy as a wolf, a most loathsome, cowardly animal, and he'll be pleased as all get out.

Of course, no man openly admits he's a wolf. He smirks and smiles and blushes and tries to giggle it off. But he sure is proud.

The dictionary defines "wolf" as a fierce, rapacious, destructive beast—or person. None of that fits the New York *canis lupus*.

He is not fierce; he traps his prey with gentle wiles. He is not rapacious, being satisfied with one at a time. (But every day is a different time.) And he is not so destructive.

The subject of wolves has been written about ad nauseam, and to most people it's an old and tedious joke. Yet, nowhere in the world save possibly Hollywood, are male wolves so much a part of the scene as in afterdark New York.

Here, wolfing has developed into an art, and though grandma's girl, after she's been around any time at all, spots the species immediately, tradition demands that she permit him to pursue and subdue her, wolf-fashion, and never let on she's wise to his act. Wolves are very sensitive.

Though there are more femmes in Gotham than in any other city on earth, it takes much ingenuity to stalk the Little Red Riding Hood here. There are no forest paths. It's the best-lighted place on earth—when John L. Lewis keeps his hands off. It is against the law to flirt on the streets of New York. He who would try it in public places, such as theatres or the subway, will get a punch in the nose if he doesn't land in the hoose-gow.

There are so many wolves in Manhattan that, even if the entire female population of Scranton, with Reading and Mauch Chunk thrown in, were transplanted here, they wouldn't cross the path of 1 per cent of our predatory males.

But here it takes specific knowledge and specialized scheming to perfect a pick-up. We have few social clubs and fewer church festivals, where you can meet the squabs in small towns. There are no corner drugstores with juke boxes to drop in on after school. People don't ask motorists for a lift here, and motorists don't give 'em.

None but professionals work cocktail lounges and hotel lobbies. Sailors provide too much competition on Riverside Drive. There are no cabaret hostesses or so-called "B Girls." It's illegal for the headwaiter to introduce you to a cutie in the show, or for you to sit out with her even if you know her or can get her to invite you.

So, where do wolves whistle? Shhh! We spent many sleepless nights gathering the info. Paste it in your hat. It tells where our choicest chickens perch.

CHORINES: If you see a plain-looking gal, sans make-up, in slacks or cheap dress, breakfasting at the fountain of a drugstore near Broadway at 5 P.M., she's a show girl. Favorite spot is Hanson's, 51st and Seventh Avenue.

Those who live on the East Side play the Belmont-Plaza drugstore. They're back again between shows for dinner at the fountain, once more, after the show, when they sip coffee with one eye peeled for a musician, press agent or other Main Stem character. When the kids are really left flat, they frequently go bowling. Many patronize the Roxy alley.

MODELS: You can always spot a "pro" model. She's usually slender, hipless, has small features, carries her make-up in a man's hat-box. Powers girls tea at the fountain in Grand Central Palace; the Conover beauts patronize the cocktail lounge of the Roosevelt Hotel; Thornton's youngsters make their headquarters at the Liggett fountain, 43d and Lexington Avenue. Smart wolves know you can always find models at cocktail time in Armando's.

But we must tell you about the famed Round Table at John Perona's El Morocco, expensive East Side rendezvous. The table is so situated that the town's aging and more prosperous squab-hunters, like Macoco, who congregate at it nightly can case the door and ogle the bims brought in by younger and more energetic men. The bald and graying Knights of the Table Round select and signal, and by a method we cannot detail, get phone numbers.

* * *

Many of the most successful wolves do not drink. Alcohol is a hurdle in the chase. The trick is to let her do the imbibing.

It is strictly unprofessional for a wolf to pay a girl, ever. Anyone can pay.

Married wolves are debarred if they lie and say they're single or pull the old one about being misunderstood. Naturally, the town's top lupos are married.

* * *

WISDOM OF A WHITE WAY WOLF:
"Woman is like your shadow. Follow it, it flies you. Fly, it will pursue you!"—Ben Jonson.

* * *

When your doll starts showing an interest in another, don't agree with her appraisal of him. If you make it too easy for her to leave you for another, she won't— and you're stuck with her.

* * *

Fastest way to a doll's heart is not through protestations of love and undying affection. Keep her laughing, bud. That's the block buster.

* * *

Guys who give seldom get.

203

It's tough to romance a chorine while she's rehearsing for a new show. Hard-boiled dance directors are mayhem on love life.

* * *

When you have a date with a chorus doll and she keeps you waiting after a show—being last to leave the dressing room—it can mean one of two things. Either she's so thrilled to be going out with you, she primps more than usual. Or she's so bored and unconcerned she stalls to the last minute. Make up your mind.

* * *

Dames that pull the share-a-date gag are carbolic acid. Give 'em the air when they do this: The evening is half over; suddenly she remarks that she's got to go. "Why, dear," says she, "I told you earlier I had this date, but to show you how much I care for you I ducked him all these hours to spend them with you." The malarkey!

* * *

When a doll tells you she couldn't get a job in the cabaret chorus because the boss tried to get fresh with her, it's a phony. There's such a shortage of pretty femmes who dance that managers would rather hire them than make love to them—paying up to $100 a week, two shows a night, six days a week—and saying "Please."

* * *

Don't try to start a conversation with the pretty pigeon at the end of the bar. She's the bartender's bim and no stray can steal her.

* * *

When your doll excuses herself to go to the powder room—a few minutes after she nods to the sleek dark musician—watch out that she doesn't give you a powder.

23. THE NOTED AND THE NOTORIOUS

A BIG shot is just a pain in the neck to the average New Yorker, who has seen them all and seen them come and go. He is a nuisance who has to be endured; a nuisance because he gets in front of the line, has the best tables, blocks entrances with his car and generally makes himself obnoxious.

New York reeks with very important people. Most, of course, aren't celebrities. They mind their own business and try to forget their fame.

But, if a New Yorker can take or leave his notables, a muzhik can't. Next to the Empire State and Radio City, V.I.P.'s are the tallest things on his agenda, and if it's your hard luck to nursemaid one, you've got to take him to one place where he can feed his obsession. And many celebs are only too anxious to oblige.

There's a prosperous firm in town called Celebrity Service, which, for a fee, advises just which celebrities are where and when. Subscribers, in addition to newspapers, press agents and high pressure salesmen, often include fan clubs.

If the sidewalk outside a public place is filled with moronic-looking imbeciles of both sexes, grasping autograph books and candid cameras, it's a pretty safe bet someone whom they consider important is inside or expected.

Exhibitionistic hams love it and you can find them

with their silly smirking faces at any hour around the clock.

These are some of the places where they hang out:

Algonquin Hotel—Lunch place of the la-de-dah literary set.

Barberry Room—Socialites, for dinner.

Blair House—Broadway and sports figures.

Colony—Top money mob, for lunch and dinner.

Copacabana—Show and sport crowd, at midnight and 2 A.M.

Copa Lounge—Show, radio, sport and press crowd, 12:30 to 4 A.M.

El Boraccho—Show, screen and society glamor gals, at dinner.

El Morocco—Top movie stars, international society, rich wolves, Duke and Duchess of Windsor. Dinner until 4 A.M.

Larue—Social climbers.

Leon & Eddie's—Ditto, Sundays, after midnight.

Lindy's (old)—Sporting and racing crowd, lunch and dinner.

Lindy's (new)—Song-writers and comedians, dinner and after theatre.

Luchow's—Tammany politicos, Mencken and Nathan, opera and theatrical.

Moore's—Movie executives and stars, sports, political and Broadway headliners.

Reuben's—Broadway mob, after 4 A.M.

Sardi's—The drama (pronounced draymah) bunch at lunch and dinner and after theatre.

Stork Club—Politicians, columnists—Walter Winchell, always—producers and movie bunch, lunch, cocktails, dinner, until 4 A.M.

Toots Shor's—Broadway, especially radio, and sporting bunch for lunch and dinner.

Twenty-One—Hollywood, Broadway and semi-society, for lunch and dinner.

Other places where celebrities can be viewed include the Metropolitan Opera House, especially on opening nights, when all the sables, stomachers and high hats turn out.

Almost every theatrical opening brings out a few celebs, though only at events like the première of an expensive musical comedy or a show with Katharine Cornell, the Lunts or Tallulah Bankhead, do you find more than the regulars.

24. THERE IS NO SOCIETY

IF THIS title seems an overstatement, you may have something. But, as far as your eye can see, it is almost categorically true.

There is a Social Register, published and revised annually. Its standards for selection are vague and the private corporation which sets them doesn't play according to its own precedents. Its principal excuses for continued existence are that it pays off, as every snob in town feels it is an essential household article, and it is the sweetest sucker list ever compiled for peddlers, panders, climbers and promoters.

The younger generation of what was once New York society has gotten largely out of hand. Its typical proponent is Gloria Vanderbilt di Cicco Stokowski, who in her teens disported herself at bars, heavily made up, one wedgie on the rail and a foot-long cigarette holder between fingers with crimson mandarin nails. To make the picture perfect, her then-beloved mother was drinking with her.

Debutantes (who rarely have debuts any more) are largely silk-lined bobby soxers. They wear slacks and sweaters out loud and mingle with tea-dancers and gin-garglers in the more expensive but no more exclusive drop-ins.

The musty, crusty Old Guard is dwindling with death and high taxes. The few who have retained their aristocratic bearing go deeper and deeper into seclusion. But even they are smudged with the sins of modernity which penetrate all walls and past all butlers. Not so long ago, one of our dozen foremost real society matrons was committed to an insane asylum. The husband of an equally blue-blooded top-drawer grand dame was beaten to death by her gigolo when he walked in on them.

The in-betweeners, neither young nor old, make pitiful pretense of youthfulness, dance until they are lame and find dignity too old-fashioned for words—the kind of words they use.

Many women born to social position are horning into politics, not a few radical. It's smart to talk red and the son of the late head of J. P. Morgan & Company is one of the loudest of this contingent.

Divorces among the social names are becoming as commonplace as they are in Hollywood.

As a backwash of the war, New York was invaded by many rich refugees and stranded titled bums. The latter found doors wide open for them.

What is left of Inanity Fair is on view rarely and only in a few spots. Great palaces have been razed or turned into dressmakers' shops or offices. Increased real estate values, hardships with help, murderous income and inheritance taxes and the disinclination of the younger members to follow the old and more gracious ways have made mausoleums of the mansions.

When these fortresses of fashion fell, society went underground. A few Knickerbocker clans, from hidden retreats, still resist attempts at intrusion by war profiteers, black marketeers and that mixed miscellany of the gossip columns—Café Society. Contrary to general belief, that is not a new institution, though for generations it was regarded from above in about the same light as a daughter of a good family who had borne twins out of wedlock.

It originated toward the end of the golden 90's, and its father was the esoteric Harry Lehr, successor to Ward McAllister, social arbiter supreme, creator of the great Mrs. William Astor's sacred 400.

Lehr had at one time been the kingpin of those since-vanished Americans, the wine (champagne) agents. It never got out of his blood, though he lofted into the social stratosphere. Perhaps as a prank or caprice or a reversion to type, on a Sunday night he induced Mrs. Astor to attend a dinner he gave at Sherry's, then at Fifth Avenue and 44th Street. That night Café Society was born.

Next morning, a newspaper published this astonishing lead:

"What are we coming to? Mrs. Astor at Sherry's table d'hôte! I never dreamt it would be given to me to gaze on the face of an Astor in a public dining room."

Next day, all the newspapers featured the epoch-making feast. One society editor wrote:

"When I saw Mrs. Astor in coquettish raiment of white satin, with the tiniest headdress, at Sherry's, dos-à-dos almost with Lillian Russell, I could scarcely believe my eyes. She seemed to enjoy it and nodded her head to the ragtime tunes. She wore her famous pearls and was a stunning sight."

Lehr was a crony of Tom Wanamaker, who owned

an apartment above Sherry's. He gave Harry the use of a beautiful suite and arranged for him to eat on the cuff in the café and entertain friends there, likewise. His historic dinner to Mrs. Astor was a shill job, to break the ice for social patronage. Night clubs follow the same device today to pump up brilliant opening nights.

Mrs. Astor undoubtedly had no suspicion of Lehr's object, but she gave the royal nod to the first big break in the fences, which eventually permitted an infiltration of Manhattan Okies into her own 400, which expanded the circle so widely that with every year it meant less and less as it grew more and more.

Perhaps the most conspicuous disintegration is visible at a glance at the Metropolitan Opera House. Première nights in the golden days were glittering spectacles, with the women of the Astor, Vanderbilt, Drexel, Gould and other proud dynasties wearing Paris gowns and radiant tiaras, and the newspapers covering the show avidly.

Today such events are drab. Anybody with the coin can buy a box in the Diamond Horseshoe. Night club managers, Broadway gamblers, cloak-and-suit salesmen entertain where formerly only meticulously screened millionaires basked in their own glory, a thousand sets of glasses trained on them from the seats of the lowly. Now strangers in business suits and women in frocks tilt back in the front chairs, originally reserved for ladies only, and rest their feet on the storied railing.

Among the last top-name regulars were Mrs. Cornelius Vanderbilt and her sister-in-law, Mrs. Orme Wilson, who shared Box 3 on different nights. Newport's famous spinster sisters, Edith and Maude Wetmore, occasionally occupy their Box 5. The Duchess de Talleyrand, née Anna Gould, retains her box, but rarely uses it. The Morgan family gave up theirs seasons ago. Most of the ladies who own rich gems no longer wear them—they're afraid of stick-ups.

The most conspicuous display is put on by Ganna Walska, who has a box on the north—the unfashionable—side. Wearing emeralds as large as limes, she is rococo in dress and demeanor and is usually attended by minor diplomats and her latest husband. She never made society, though she married one millionaire and two multi-multimillionaires. The first, which was her second, was an elderly New York physician to whom she went because she thought a growth in her throat interfered with her ambition to be a diva. He didn't cure her throat, but he married her, conveniently died and left her a home and her first million. This girl, who had sung in mid-European cabarets, was soon pursued by Harold McCormick (then married to the daughter of John D. Rockefeller); and Alexander Smith Cochran, even wealthier, the Yonkers carpet king.

Ganna decided to take a trip to Europe and both her suitors made the boat. McCormick was still married, so she took Cochran, who spent a fortune on repeated efforts here and abroad to make her a prima donna. When he failed, she blew him for McCormick, who had gotten his divorce and taken time out for a monkey-gland operation. McCormick was the foremost subsidizer and patron of the Chicago Opera Company, one

213

of the principal heirs to the McCormick harvester fortune. But he couldn't get her in that troupe and she soon waltzed out on him. (She was born with some unpronounceable Polish name and was nicknamed "Walska," meaning "waltzer," because she sang waltz songs to the accompaniment of a gypsy fiddler in Budapest.)

When last heard from, she was being sued for alimony by her sixth husband, a yoga practitioner who told her that his mysterious powers would bring forth her voice. She said she had been persuaded to believe that while she stood on her head.

First nights of old brought forth beautiful Mrs. George Gould, the former Edith Kingdon, and her friends. Now the lobbies are jammed with cigarette smokers overflowing to the sidewalks, and police reporters recognize more patrons than can the society reporters.

A recent première saw raffish exhibitionism that would have shamed Whitechapel fishwives.

Betty Henderson, a dowager past 70, in the opera bar, planted a leg on a table, showing more than plenty, and shouted, "What has Dietrich got that I haven't got?" She was probably plastered and she is a Newport top-drawer hostess, worth dozens of millions.

Another elderly jewel-rack walked the balcony during intermission, puffing a big, black cigar. Maybe she was trying to smoke herself sober.

One matron arrived with two bodyguards, who stalked and sat on either side of her, making even more conspicuous her cables of pearls and her movie-marquee display of diamonds.

But the upper crust still exists.

The great private ballrooms are no more, so the fashionables give dances and receptions at the Colony Club (not to be confused with the Colony Restaurant). For women only, this is one of the last stands of exclusiveness—so snazzy that non-members, guests, must enter by the side door. Only those who belong may use the Park Avenue portal or the main elevator within.

The Union and Knickerbocker Clubs are as snooty as the day they were founded. To increase income they instituted ladies' nights, when members may invite wives, daughters and guests to dine. The Metropolitan Club, founded by the first J. P. Morgan for the rich but outré rejected by the Union, has let down its bars, as have other smart clubs.

The Horse Show was another brilliant event in the golden age, but blue-blooded humans don't patronize it as enthusiastically as before. Fashionable women who do now affect sports togs. Those who cling to dressy traditions are stared at curiously.

In the eras of rubberneck wagons, visitors got their money's worth. Men shouted through megaphones untruthful descriptions of famous mansions. Provincials thrilled when they reached Fifth Avenue and 57th Street. The four corners were sites of baronial citadels.

On the northwest corner stood the great château of Cornelius Vanderbilt, with its iron-grilled garden in the rear. On the northeast was the white marble residence of Mrs. Hermann Oelrichs. On the southeast was the somber castle of Collis P. Huntington, and on the southwest the Moorish-windowed retreat of William C. Whitney. Today, commercial buildings have replaced them all.

The great double mansion of Mrs. William Astor and her son, John Jacob, dominated upper Fifth Avenue at 65th Street. Its walls beheld entertainments that rivaled those of oriental potentates. Its most luxurious feature was a huge bathtub, carved from a single block of Carrara marble, with gold spigots shaped like dolphins' heads. Mrs. Jack Astor, nee Ava Willing, America's most celebrated society beauty, now Lady Ribblesdale, laved herself there in eau de cologne. The architecturally impressive Temple Emanu-el now stands where all this was.

The white mansion of Mrs. Oliver Belmont, at 51st Street and Madison Avenue, is now the Administration Building of the Catholic Archdiocese. The brownstone Jay Gould town house, at Fifth Avenue and 47th Street, where shouting thousands clamored for the life of the Wall Street operator on historic Black Friday, is a furniture store. The famous Bertie Goelet home, a block away, was recently razed.

The largest private residence in the city, the brownstone palace at 640 Fifth Avenue, where Mr. Cornelius Vanderbilt entertained royalty and the other elect, was sold to the English Astors and has since been demolished. Its famed marble mantelpieces and interior decorations were auctioned to Hollywood producers. An office building was erected on its site. Mrs. Vanderbilt, undaunted, carries on in a smaller house at 1048 Fifth Avenue.

On the upper stretch of this boulevard are the magnificent ménages of Mrs. Mary Duke Biddle, Dr. A. Hamilton Rice, Mrs. Hamilton McTwombly, Mrs. William Hayward, Julia Berwind, Mrs. W. Watts Sherman, and the garden-enclosed, garishly grandiose showplace of the late Andrew Carnegie. The Carnegies are not gregarious and few fashionables have seen the interior. Set in between them, in a regal mansion once owned by Whitney Warren, a society architect, and designer of Grand Central Terminal, was an all-night "bottle club" that dispensed liquid refreshment after closing time to a favored few.

On Riverside Drive, the gingerbread château of the late Charles M. Schwab which long stood empty has also been torn down. The Schwabs were not social, but musical. Their Sunday afternoon concerts when Melba, Tetrazzini and other prima donnas sang, were discussed even in Europe.

At 1 East 78th Street, on the corner of Fifth Avenue, is the white marble palace of Mrs. James B. Duke, mother of Doris. This great house has a magnificent collection of 18th century English paintings and drawings.

The Harrison Williamses live at 1130 Fifth Avenue. The beautiful Mona entertains there against a distinguished background of paneled rooms, her portrait by Dali, and several Goyas.

The Byron Foys live at 60 East 93rd Street, in one of the finest houses in the city. Built by Mrs. Graham Fair

217

Vanderbilt, it has the most beautiful French 18th century paneling. On its walls are portraits by great masters as well as family portraits painted by Simon Elwes.

But most socialites live in vast apartment houses or hotels. To see them in the flesh, one can peep in several restaurants. Tops is the Colony, on East 61st Street, just off Madison. It serves wonderful food at wonderful prices. Strangers find it difficult to get reservations. If one does, he will be far back, in the main room. Many regulars prefer it there, though, and you may land next to Winthrop Rockefeller, Baron Maurice de Rothschild, Clark Gable, or, while she was here, you might have encountered Princess Martha of Norway.

Table No. 1, at the right of the entrance, was long reserved for the William K. Vanderbilts. After his death, his widow never returned. Now one is apt to find at this spot the Duke and Duchess of Windsor, Mme. Frances, the Alfred Sloanes or young Lord Lascelles. Table No. 21 is bachelor-girl Beth Leary's hangout. At No. 14, Mrs. George U. Harris and her charming daughter, Lucille, are on view. No. 34 is where Elsa Maxwell, Clare Boothe Luce or Dorothy Thompson sit, but not together. Table No. 4b is given to the Vincent Astors, to Lady Furness, or to society reporters.

Voisin is smart, but far more conservative, and none of the faces would mean anything to the uninitiated.

To El Morocco goes the International Set.

The remaining few aristocrats bide their time, believing and hoping for a revival which will never come. But they are curious. Mrs. Cornelius Vanderbilt visited the Stork Club ONCE. Mrs. Hamilton McK. Twombly went to dinner at the Monte Carlo ONCE. And that vital nonagenarian, Colonel Creighton Webb, has been to a night club *twice*.

Society departments still appear in the newspapers, a habit the editors fear to shake off. But their content is mostly betrothals and weddings of people few know —no charity balls, no formal functions, no musical soirées, no tally-ho outings, polo or fox hunts in season.

In another year or two, a new superior set may arise —composed of union labor leaders, rising reds and affluent Africans.

Until then, Society will go like the gallant G.A.R.— doomed by the toll of time.

25. HOODLUMS' HIERARCHY

When this chapter first appeared in print in 1948, they said we were nuts. The following year, when we wrote Chicago Confidential, *we expanded on the subject of the organized underworld. That made our critics hysterical.*

But the findings of the Kefauver Committee, which got its original inspiration from these books, proved how right we were. In fact, the Senate Crime Committee's final report was practically a plagiarism of Chicago Confidential, *and* Washington Confidential.

*T*HE RATTLE of the sawed-off tommy-gun, the whining whistle of the leaden slug and the thud of its impact against flesh and bone no longer are the sound effects in the orchestration of the gangsters' theme song.

In the last decade an extraordinary metamorphosis has come over the characters who saw their big years of glamor and of terror during Prohibition and for a spell after repeal.

In truth, there are no gangsters, and there are no mobs. Yet, today's underworld figures cast a far wider shadow and wield an incalculably greater influence on the life of the nation and its principal city.

Except for a few shabby neighborhood ruffians in squabbles about penny-ante rackets, such as fish-peddling, shakedowns of storekeepers, enforcing collections for double sawbuck loan sharks and similar bagatelles, the old and happy habits of killing each other have evaporated.

Everything is now organized into an institution a hundred times the proportion of any outfit dramatized by Raft and Robinson, including the empire of Al Capone, which is represented as a minor element in the set-up that grew out of it all.

Today we have the Syndicate!

Let it not be supposed that the hoodlums have gone straight. The Syndicate is almost entirely bossed by ex-convicts whose roots are in the lowest and most violent soil, where originated malignant morasses of the dirty trades that made America notorious around the world.

But they have grown up. They are fat and rich, they have wives who belong to clubs and children going to the best colleges. And they have brains.

These brains are like none other, because they combine the shrewdness and unscrupulous ruthlessness of high-powered criminals with the hired skill and concentration of first-line lawyers, accountants, business sharks and tax specialists.

Their operations and their holdings now run into the multimillions. And they range from the filthy numbers swindle in the Negro sections of most large cities to chains of America's finest and biggest hotels, a building of their own in the heart of Wall Street, distilleries, breweries, real estate worth up to $5,000 a front foot, blue-chip stocks and bonds galore, night clubs and restaurants and the structures that house them.

At the same time, they juggle the Italian lottery, a gold mine which has had comparatively little publicity, and which flourishes in every city that has slums; call-girl vice, the last survivor of the woman traffic in New

York and a prolific source of profit; the international narcotics trade, with a world-wide organization for supply abroad and distribution in the United States, which probably turns over more than $1,000,000 a day here; almost complete monopoly of American book-making, the slot-machine business where they can put on the fix, and the lion's share of the gambling in Florida and Saratoga in season, in Nevada all the time and in various large centers where and when they can operate with comparative safety through political connections.

This strange hybrid of respectability and lawless monopoly was really born of Al Capone's conviction on income-tax frauds.

It shocked the mobsters, who had thought themselves immune, into a realization that any one of them, without an hour's notice, could be tapped for Alcatraz. Capone's defense was childish and completely without preparation for a man who had proven himself not only big and bold, but crafty and cautious, when he had weighed the odds for and against himself.

There was in plain relief a record of big expenditures which he could not controvert and against which he could not prove income—that is, income which he had reported—and this was no trial for bootlegging or murder, but strictly a tax-evasion indictment.

It is an axiom accepted by thieves that you can't do business with Uncle Whiskers.

There were a number of meetings, in Chicago, New York and elsewhere, and the principal subject was:

"How can we beat that Treasury rap?"

The government does not usually prosecute where there is a confusion or a possible one as to tax liability. It reviews a return, examines books, asks questions, snoops around and notifies the subject that his questionnaire was faulty and that he owes so and so much on such and such findings. He then pays up, or sometimes settles and is even given a leeway of time to make restitution. The worst that happens to him is that he kicks in.

These conferees represented leading mobsters from New York and Brooklyn, Newark, Philadelphia, Miami, New Orleans, Chicago, Detroit, Los Angeles, San Francisco and other points which do not seem important, but for strategic or geographical reasons developed gang personalities.

It was then and there decided that, instead of jamming their thousand- and ten-thousand-dollar bills into strong boxes, they would form a pool and invest in sound enterprises. In these they got actual, tangible, negotiable securities. They engaged the best management, often retaining the executives of properties they bought.

Then came the war and everything flourished and multiplied—everything honest and dishonest.

Their assets snowballed. Now they run into incalculable figures.

Every member has his exact "piece"—from the take of a prostitute summoned in the night, to the income on Park Avenue, State Street and Hollywood Boulevard frontage.

Any man who owns 2 per cent is a millionaire. The

principal participant is said to own 7½ per cent and he is now the richest man in Italy. He is, of course, Charles "Lucky" Luciano.

When Luciano, a swarthy Sicilian with a drooping eye, who had been a pickpocket, a pimp, a collector, a gun-toter for his betters and in time the top racketeer of the United States, was convicted by District Attorney Tom Dewey, it was said that he was railroaded and that he was guilty of everything except what he was convicted for—peddling women.

He was guilty of them all and that, too. But Dewey, with his eye looking far ahead, realized that this was the most spectacular path and he took it and followed it through.

It was the same Dewey, as governor, who shortened Luciano's sentence at Dannemora under circumstances never plausibly explained. It was published that Luciano had provided the government, then at war, with priceless information about the Italian underworld, which had helped us in the invasion. It was even bruited that he would get a medal of honor. This was all pure hokum, invented by the paid press agent of the syndicate in New York, which maintains a year-round public-relations employe who earns his $300 a week if he manages to get in one choice item, such as the above, in a year.

It was no political deal, which also was intimated, but which is as erroneous as the balderdash about Luciano's service to his adopted country.

Luciano got an excessive sentence, running up to 30 years. It was not contemplated that he would ever sit out all of that. The Italians, who are rapidly overtaking the Irish as the leading power in Tammany and in Republican councils as well, had put on heavy pressure to get amnesty for the little mug, who was the head of the Sicilian Society in the United States, a branch of the ancient Mafia.

After Luciano was deported, he turned up in Havana.

This was kept out of the newspapers for a while, but the entire syndicate was notified and there was a concentration in the Cuban capital, where 36 rooms had been engaged in Havana's leading hotel.

Meanwhile, the FBI and Federal Bureau of Narcotics tapped his phone-calls to the mainland and definitely established that he was still in undisputed command of the multifarious and nefarious operations of the infamous Unione Siciliano.

Columnist Robert Ruark sprung the story in a column which appeared in the second section of his newspaper and was treated as minor information. But the fact that he had seen Luciano holding court in the Havana Casino, surrounded by glamor gals, underworld and Hollywood celebrities, including Ralph Capone, the Fischetti Brothers and Frank Sinatra caused a national sensation, as a result of which the United States government formally complained to the Cuban government that Luciano's presence on the nearby island meant a big development in the dope business of the United States. Washington had the goods.

Cuba thereupon deported him back to Sicily, where at this writing he is dispensing charity and undoubtedly buying and scheming great influence in public affairs.

During his incarceration, his dividends as well as his crooked profits were meticulously deposited to his credit. There was some difficulty transferring money to him in Italy during the last year of the war, and in that period some $2,000,000 accrued to him; that sum was brought to him in cash on a Pan-American clipper from Miami to Havana and carried in the hand of a well-known crooner of Italian extraction, with underworld connections past and present, guarded by two of the Fischettis, cousins of Al Capone.

The New York manipulator for Lucky, who visited him while he was held at Ellis Island for deportation, is Frank Costello. He is now the mightiest of the syndicate personnel, with an uncanny genius for mixing into highly important affairs with bigwigs in various spheres.

Costello also was born in Sicily, came to New York in his youth, had some juvenile delinquency troubles and did a stretch before he was out of his teens. He was part and parcel of gangster developments in a small way until his talents brought him to the top.

He was engaged in the slot-machine business in New York until the late Fiorello LaGuardia had his one-armed bandits smashed by police axes. Costello, teaming with "Dandy Phil" Kastel, who also had counted the bars on a cell, took a trial trip to Louisiana, then the one-man dominion of Huey Long.

They say a million dollars passed into the hands of the Huey Long inner group—and not a bad investment, for the first year's profits, reported for Federal taxes, exceeded $1,200,000. Anyway, the Louisiana legislature voted a bill legalizing slot machines, and Costello and Kastel organized several inter-involved corporations with innocent names to run them. There was practically no competition—and very little shooting; Long simply passed the word around that the concession belonged to these two gentlemen from New York.

As a concrete example of how the tax situation is manipulated by intricate items of overlaying accounts, it was shown when Costello was hauled up for taxes apparently due, that the slot machines belonged to one corporation, that they were operated by a second, which rented the locations from a third.

Costello eventually settled for $600,000 cash. Among other little entries about which the government inquired were payments of $200,000 a year to each of his wife's two brothers, as salaries in different slot-machine corporations. This transparent cover-up was laughable —but it was judged not criminal. Costello pleaded that he had been misadvised—excuse it, please—and he wrote a check.

This is only a ripple on the ocean of hundreds, probably thousands, of holding companies organized in various states and under various directorships and local laws, through which flow the vast garnerings of the syndicate from coast to coast, with an accounting system which in any emergency can explain and make good any entry, and thus avoid the peril of the penitentiary.

There is an intercommunicating liaison among the lawyers, many of whom are engaged for their exclusive services by the year, and all supervising the main channels and watching hawklike to guard against letting their employers become involved in actionable tax delinquencies.

As for all other matters, they can be handled locally. The syndicate owns plenty of judges, strong men in both parties and great fluid assets. It is no secret that money can square anything in the United States.

Luciano was no peanut when Dewey ruined him. But there are few Deweys. And Luciano had not yet learned to cover his tracks. The money came in so fast and his drag was so good, he felt immune, but Tom Dewey wanted to be President of the United States, and Lucky hadn't thought of that.

Luciano had been taken for a ride in the orthodox manner, between two executioners, and had come out alive. They left him for dead in a lonely spot, but he beat it.

After that he felt that nothing could break him.

Like Samson, he was betrayed by infatuation for a doll. She was Gay Orlova, a fabulously beautiful, but plump, blonde White Russian refugee, who had come to Broadway and Earl Carroll's choruses by way of Turkey.

Said by Carroll to be "the sexiest gal who ever worked for me," Gay quickly found a protector in the late Theus Munds, rich and elderly Wall Street broker, who went whole hog with diamonds, furs and limousines.

During the Florida season of 1935, Gay appeared as a featured show girl in the floor show Carroll presented in the flamboyant Palm Island Casino, then operated by Bill Dwyer, a Prohibition-time big-shot rumrunner, on Al Capone's private island.

There she met Luciano. Lucky, who had had the pick of girls, never had had one so glamorous—or amorous. He moved right in.

Gay was proud of her conquest. When asked by one of your reporters, "What about Munds?" she replied, "Oh, Theus is O.K. But all he's got is money. Lucky, he's sinister!"

When that was printed, it was the first intimation Dewey's detectives had of the romance. When Gay returned to New York, they tapped her wires, and thereby traced Luciano to Hot Springs, Arkansas, where he was hiding out.

After Lucky's conviction, Uncle Sam deported Gay as an undesirable alien. When last heard of she was a Paris mannequin, still beautiful, still in love with Luciano, still bitter at your reporters—and trying to get a passport to Italy.

His conviction was another lesson to his kind. It showed them that, with all their accumulated power, they were not sure of their liberty.

Luciano had conducted his vice operations from a duplex suite in the Waldorf Towers. These activities were traced right into his two manicured hands. The syndicate came to the conclusion that that, too, must be changed.

Now the important stockholders delegate everything

illegal. In one season the outfit netted $6,000,000 in Miami gambling houses. But these were all run by stooges, few of whom knew to whom the money eventually went, and none of whom knew how or where it went—into corporations with strange and remote names, into sinking funds, reserves, depreciation allocations and undivided profits.

Corporations can be sued and can be taken, but they cannot be locked in a prison.

That, briefly, is the story of the gangsters' progress, one of the biggest-monied combinations in the nation. That is the reason why the shootings have stopped and top men are no longer put on the spot.

"Bugsy" Siegel and Binaggio, slain after this chapter first appeared in print, were exceptions. Benny, who got his nickname because the boys said he was "nuts," had threatened to blow the whistle on the syndicate when Luciano refused to bail him out of his $6,500,000 white-elephant gambling casino-hotel in Las Vegas, Nevada.

He was put on the spot because he refused to be "organized"; preferred old-fashioned gang methods learned when he was the No. 1 torpedo for Murder, Inc. Binaggio, too, double-crossed the boys.

No independent operator can scratch the surface. Competition isn't even a hearty joke. The boys have everything so tightly tied up, they work so far ahead and have so many trained eyes and ears, that they can take long vacations, enjoy a hangover as well as the next man and sleep in reasonable security under silk canopies in silk pajamas.

26. HELLO SUCKER!

THREE different movie outfits, at three different times, took the trouble to consult with Jack Lait about authentic incidents in the life of Texas Guinan. He gave freely and at great length in response. We later saw "Incendiary Blonde," supposed to be based on her life. It wasn't a bad picture. But it wasn't a good Guinan.

Tex was hardly incendiary, and wasn't even a blonde by nature. The only three men in her life were—first, a quiet New England artist; second, a sedate California writer; and third, in later days, a bookkeeper, no less, who used to beat her up and who scrammed with a lot of her assets.

Texas and Lait were good friends back in 1913, when she was making two-reel, two-gun westerns. That's when she acquired the "Texas" handle. Her name was Mamie. She had a little house near Hollywood, with Lottie Pickford and Mabel Normand. Lew Cody, Paul Armstrong and Lait would drive out there to play stud poker. Texas came east to joint a musical show. Abe Erlanger, king of the legit, went soft for a little pug nose in the chorus and took Texas' song away and gave it to the youngster. To make it worse, he wanted Texas to support her with an obligato. Lait stood on the stage of the Illinois Theatre, Chicago, when Tex told Erlanger off pretty in the presence of the entire troupe.

She was fired instanter and barred from every branch of theatricals except vaudeville. Lait wrote her an act, with four people and a horse. At the climax, Tex on the horse leaped in through the window and saved the post office from being robbed. Her name wasn't good enough for the big time, and she played the Loew circuit. Transportation ate up most of the salary. So Tex got a job as a hostess in the Beaux Arts, New York, opposite Bryant Park, high up by elevator, sort of a secluded spot after the uptown speaks were emptied. There her personality caught on.

Larry Fay, the sentimental gangster, had gone mad over a lovely little ingénue whose name shall not be mentioned, because it might embarrass her and it wasn't her fault. Larry pestered her so, she ran away to Florida and took a cheap night club engagement. This gave Larry a big idea, which made Texas Guinan, quite inadvertently.

The Friars Club, about to open its own building, was moving out of its temporary quarters on 45th Street, near Sixth Avenue. Fay leased the building for five years. His plan was to set up a magnificent club which he thought would lure back to New York the gal he was nuts about, if he offered her star billing and a big salary. He hired Tex as emcee, with a heavy guarantee. He called it the El Fey Club so it could be identified with him and still not carry his name, which was on record where it wouldn't help. He began frantically telephoning the girl in Florida. She turned him down and after the first call refused to answer. So here he was, stuck with a five-year lease on a five-story building and a contract with Guinan.

Here comes the most interesting incident, which has never been truly told and which has been untruly told for years everywhere.

As each show went on, Larry would stand in the extreme rear, where it was dark and where he—always in plain blue serge suit, white silk shirt and black windsor tie—was inconspicuous. As Texas would mount her chair (that was how she worked) she would look across the long room at him. And, thinking of the lease, her pay, the flop of his romantic objective, she would cast a glance right over the heads of the audience and call out—to him—"Hello, sucker!"

Through some phenomenal human quirk, every other sucker in between thought it was addressed to him. And, as strangely, every man liked it. It became her trademark. Long after Larry passed out of her picture and was killed on a New Year's morning, she still featured it—his only monument.

Texas played to a strange conglomeration—Wall Street, the world of art and letters, the Blue Book lorgnette set, New York's usual concentration of out-of-town buyers, plus never-failing underworlders. These were all paying guests. There was very little passed out on the cuff in any of her deadfalls. There were very few beefs about atrociously phony "champagne" at $35 a bottle, and some of the bootleggers who made her Scotch and gin at perhaps $1 a quart came to her dives and paid $15 a quart for their own hogwash.

There was something in that "Hello, sucker!" which softened up a man and made him what she called him. She always had a flock of lovely young girls, but no customer ever got closer to them than seeing them on the floor. It was no place to pick up one on short notice. Texas watched over her kids like Diana guarded the doves on Olympus. Many a contented matron, perhaps now turning 40, may remember what a demon chaperon she was.

"Give the little girl a great big hand!" But that was all. Not a great big car; not even a sandwich.

She never got rich. She lived in a little flat on Eighth Street, which looked like a Chinese second-hand furniture store, where she had one servant. She certainly left no great sum. She dropped a wad in the stock market crash and had to hock her "ice," in which she had sunk a bucket of bucks. She had thieves and thugs for partners and, though regarded as a shrewd operator, she was taken like Armour takes a sheep. From the moment she came to work at night, until daylight, she was on her job and had no time even to look at accounts. She could well have said "Hello, sucker!" talking to herself.

But she was dynamite as a drawing card. The sappos began laughing before they came in. They greased headwaiters heavily for ringside seats in front, and a few minutes later saw tables moved in front of them. The best act she ever put on was George Raft, doing a Charleston, which lasted a minute. Ruby Keeler broke through the barrier with her beauty and tap-dancing.

Beyond this, there were practically no principals, except Guinan.

Yet, when the band struck up "I'll See You in My Dreams," her theme song, and the spotlight caught her scintillant smile and she shouted "Hello, sucker!" her customers were electrified, ecstatic. We have never known an exclamation from any person to carry the wallop that this impertinent quip packed when Guinan let go with it.

It is generally believed she got it from Wilson Mizner. Truth is, Bill Mizner got it from her!

27. NO PAIN, NO FUN

THE HOTEL HUSTLER, age-old character more or less tolerated in the best institutions, making her hunting habitat in midtown lobbies and the various "peacock alley" passages, has become a police problem on grounds other than protection of morals.

In the main hotel sectors, she spurns the wage of service. She is generally a cold, calculating crook.

Her equipment is a small bottle of white crystals, chloral hydrate, a powerful concentrated hypnotic which will knock a man completely out in 15 minutes and keep him unconscious for some dozen hours.

This method requires that she be in the man's room. She cannot take him to her own or to a neutral one, as he will wake up in due time, robbed of every nickel, his watch and ring, sometimes even some haberdashery.

A complaint, were the victim to regain consciousness anywhere but in his pro tem quarters, would set the dicks waiting for the lady to come home, if it were her place, or would convict a place that rented rooms to her as an assignation house, which in New York means lifting the license for keeps.

But, where traveling men, convention gatherers, visiting buyers and occasional migrants have accommodations, she combines in comparative safety the lure of her charms and the modus operandi of her larceny.

The flirtation is simple enough. The proposition comes in due course, usually in the cocktail lounge or

café of the hotel. The acceptance is at first hesitant—
she isn't that kind, shouldn't stay out long, but she has
taken a fancy to the stranger (after she has worked out
of him the information that he is stopping at the hotel
and isn't a permanent guest) and so, yes, she will go to
his room—unaccustomed as she is to unconventional
adventure—for a little while. He doesn't dream how
little time.

His room is not only her objective, but there is no
other retreat.

Should he want to lead her somewhere else, he is
stymied. All hotels are full up. Even if he got a handbag and tried to get into another haven with her, he
would be asked for his reservation.

There are no more loose hotels specializing in such
twosomes. In 1940, there were hundreds. Now there
isn't one. The war rush, the military police, the high
rates for legitimate rentals turned them all respectable.
They found that more profitable and kept it up.

Because of her system, she cannot take him to her
abode or to any other which he can identify after his
long snooze, even if she, a wise New York cookie, does
know some side-street bed-house where a cheating clerk
holds out a cubicle or two for quick turnovers.

So she plays quite helpless. She lives with her folks.
Unless they go to his place—well, where else?

He takes the standard precautions of the seasoned
wayfarer. He goes up alone, tells her to follow in five
minutes and walk right in.

With few exceptions, the dreaded "Get that woman
out of your room!" has gone the way of the one-buck

blue plate. Guests are still protected, but not against
their own peccadillos. The simp has pushed the little
plunger so the knob will turn from the outside. The
tough trollop, acting nervous and timid, but irresistibly
tempted, enters.

He makes a grab. Oh—he mustn't be so impulsive, so
impatient. She is jittery and fluttery—natch, since she
is doing what her breeding and better nature tell her
she should never have yielded to.

A drink—one little drink to settle the nerves—and
then—

He calls room service, even if he has a bottle in his
bag. If he has seltzer, she can drink it only with ginger
ale, or vice versa. When the waiter is called, she steps
into the bathroom on his knock, and the cluck giggles
and says he always takes two about that time of day.
The waiter says lots of customers do, it's getting to be
a national habit. For that he gets a bill instead of a
coin.

She has taken her purse into the bathroom with her,
and when she can safely return she has the knockout
dose held between the thumb and the palm of her
gloved hand—she keeps the gloves on; no fingerprints.

She sits, then remembers she has left her handker-
chief on the washstand—would he please get it? As he
turns his back, she drops the tasteless, colorless grains
into his drink, which dissolves them instantly.

They raise glasses. Here's to crime! Skoal!

If he comes over for a grab right away, she holds him
off. She wants to know—is he really married? Oh, dear,
all attractive men are! She is a grass widow. Yes, she
made a mistake, but what does a girl know when she's

18, and unworldly? How about a cigarette? Is he sure the door is locked now? He makes sure.

By this time his eyes are heavy, his hands more so. He can't understand—it's been a hard day, of course, and last night—zowie! He'll snap out of it in a minute. But he doesn't.

She has stalled until a debilitating lethargy overcomes him. He sinks back, limp. She waits a few more minutes. She pokes him. No reaction. Then she goes to work. He may still see and know what she is doing. But he is paralyzed.

She goes through him, even taking off his shoes and socks, for she has learned that many a cautious cluck hides currency there. She frisks his trousers, vest and coat. Then she scrams.

Quite a number of official beefs to the cops have completely established every move. Though only an infinitesimal percentage of the total go to the police, these average a dozen a week, mostly at East 51st Street police station, which is in the district of most top-grade hotels.

The dicks often can name the dame on description. But, if they collar her, she gives them the horselaugh. No corroboration.

After a touch in one hotel, hustlers usually move on to others, to avoid running into the victim, though when they do, little can be done about it.

Time and again, when arrests are made, the bottle of chloral hydrate is found in the suspect's handbag. That still isn't convicting evidence.

Most of the saps, of course, really are married. And they are people of some standing back home. They will lie to avoid prosecution, which would invite publicity, even when the thieving broad is caught with their watches which have their full names engraved on the cases.

The drug, without which the entire clockwork would stand still, is not too difficult to get. Chloral hydrate is a recognized and respectable anodyne, in the pharmacopoeia, prescribed for quick insensibility when a patient has convulsions, and in drastic cases as a pain-killer. It cannot be had ethically except on a physician's prescription, but there are underworld druggists as there are underworld medics, and both serve out the stuff knowing how it will be used.

An overdose can be fatal, and women who feel secure in mulcting men do not want to chance a murder rap, which would set the bulls working in full cry. So they often have the powder put up in capsules with just the right dose, and they open the gelatinous envelope, spill the contents into the hand and drop the container into the drain.

All this gives you some idea of the intensive forethought and preparation expended to turn the ancient and never-too-honorable calling from whoring to robbery.

While the two have long been associated, only of late has it become the custom not only to give the sucker no even break, but no break at all. A glib grifter in this streamlined system could work it indefinitely and retain her virtue.

Newspapers continually dig up new versions of the "meanest thief." We nominate this one!

PART THREE

THE LOWDOWN
(*Confidential!*)

28. BUT YOU'VE GOT TO GET HERE FIRST

THE trouble with most books about New York is that their authors seem to think you are already here, before you begin to read the first page.

Though this is the atomic age, with transport planes winging through the air at 400 miles an hour, no one has yet materialized a magic carpet.

We take it for granted you plan to travel by one of the conventional means: train, plane, bus, ship or car. Allowances also will be made for hitchhikers and those who ride the rods. New York is no place for those who come by motorcycle or camel or trailer. There are no trailer parks or motels or roadside rooming houses in or near the city.

At this stage of the game, we will not inquire into your motives, though later on we expect you to do a bit of soul searching—confidential—to discover in which category you fit.

If you are attracted by the glimmer of the lights or the gold of the markets, it's all the same to us. But first you've got to get here.

Choice space on de luxe trains, planes and ships will always be at a premium. It was so before the war and it is now. We assume you are coming here first class. And, coming for business or pleasure, we strongly recommend it.

If for the former, there's nothing like putting on a

front. It also helps you feel important to yourself. If for the latter, why not have all the conveniences?

* * *

If traveling by plane (and it's your first flight) try to go nonstop. You will find that once aloft, you have no sensation of flying; it's the landings and take-offs that jitter the tyro.

If you're coming by train, try to get a private bedroom. Never take anything smaller than a drawing room for two people. (Most experienced travelers demand a compartment for one.)

(INSIDE STUFF: But the prettiest gals usually travel in coach trains or on the cheaper Pullmans. Passengers on extra-fare trains are almost entirely businessmen and some couples. It is difficult to make friends on such trains as the 20th Century and the Super Chief, because most passengers keep to their rooms for the entire trip. On the other hand, those who ride the more moderately priced trains are friendlier and easier to talk to. Travel etiquette does not prevent you from talking to the sweet sister in the next seat. But if you do, you are expected to invite her into the diner and pick up her check.)

Federal and many state laws make it illegal to offer a premium for plane or train reservations. But it is no crime, of course, to tip a hotel porter liberally for securing same.

Railroad and airline employes are forbidden to accept gratuities for tickets. But, during the war, experienced travelers found a legal joker which they are still using.

If you have difficulty getting a reservation to New York, go up to your local ticket agent and say to him, "I bet you $20 you can't get me a compartment on the Century tomorrow."

He doubtless will take you up.

And, strangely enough, he will win.

* * *

Neither railroads nor inland steamship lines are curious about the lady who accompanies you into your berth, compartment or drawing room.

If you pay for and buy your ticket for two, in advance, no questions are asked, nor does the line have authority to eject you if you forgot to buy her a wedding ring.

(INSIDE STUFF: Though Pullman employes may request the lady you met on the train to leave your room, they seldom do.)

(INSIDE STUFF: It is a felony to transport females across state lines for immoral purposes.)

(INSIDE STUFF: Adultery is a felony in New York State. But there hasn't been a prosecution in more than 100 years.)

Experienced travelers carry as little baggage as possible. Furthermore (especially if you're female) you'll want to buy most of your clothes in New York.

Domestic airlines limit you to 40 pounds of luggage per person with a stiff surcharge for extras.

Tipping is not permitted on airlines and your stewardess will be insulted if you offer her one. But you are expected to remunerate the red cap porters who carry your luggage from cab to plane or airport bus.

On the contrary, your every move by train requires you to shell out.

Though most amateur travelers know they are supposed to tip red caps, Pullman porters and dining-car waiters, few realize the importance of slipping the diner steward a few bucks, five at least for a couple is usual if there are several meals.

Unless you have ridden with him before and he knows you give, you should hand him his as soon as you enter the diner for your first meal.

At a cost of a few dollars you will change your trip, especially a long one, from an experience in inferiority to one's that's at least tolerable.

The non-tipper stands in line for a table, eats only what's on the menu (if still in stock) and gets the general pushing around he deserves.

But for the tall tipper, the steward turns the car inside out, whispers of steaks, mountain trout, and front-riding seats and tables from which the parsimonious will be barred.

The warning given all prospective voyagers in naïve old days, to beware of gamblers on trains, is no longer believed generally necessary. Human nature hasn't changed, but trains have.

As already pointed out, passengers in de luxe cars keep to their rooms, whereas those who mix more are in the cheaper coach trains and therefore probably not considered bait by the predatory.

But watch your luggage in stations, especially for the old switch racket, in which the operator substitutes a bag resembling yours, stuffed with old telephone books, for your own valuable belongings.

At this writing, liquor is not sold or served to stock passengers on domestic planes except Northwest Airlines and it is against rules to tote your own hip pocket flask to drink while aloft. But no one cares if you do.

Most through trains carry club cars, in which excellent hooch is sold at moderate prices. Liquor is not sold in club cars or diners while traveling through dry states (such as Kansas) or on Sunday in many wet states (such as Pennsylvania, Ohio and Indiana).

If you can't do without your firewater, consult the ticket agent before boarding the train. Most club cars stop serving at 11 P.M., but if you tip the porter he'll provide you in advance with sufficient individual drink bottles and set-ups to keep you happy all the way.

Club cars, incidentally, are the only ones in which you can meet people on de luxe trains. If you fancy a gal sitting in one, etiquette permits you to offer a drink.

Dolls who don't want such overtures shouldn't sit in club cars alone.

Of all travelers, the bus passenger finds himself at once in the most congenial crowd and the most uncomfortable surroundings. But, for the young or the adventurous, it holds prospects seldom found in planes or trains.

Before you've gone 100 miles you are addressing the person next to you by the first name. If it should be an overnight trip, and she is cute and young, the odds are you'll be cuddling to keep warm after the lights are dimmed and the others drop off.

If it's a two-day trip, you'll be engaged to marry before you reach the Hudson, and probably will have to.

The experts on such things tell us you find the prettiest girls (and handsomest men) on buses.

The dolls from the far, small places, who come to Gotham for gold and glory, to be chorines or models, seldom have more than a few dollars, which must be stretched to the limit. The bus is the economy way.

Joe Russell, a New York press agent, has achieved some local fame for usually being the first to escort the latest young innocent beaut in town.

We investigated to find out how he got them and learned that he made a practice of haunting the bus terminals and talking to the pretty ones who alighted.

He asked them if they came to get in show business and usually got an affirmative answer. Then he offered to help them, and sometimes did, but not before he had a chance to show them off before the wolves at the hot spots.

Many of these gals advanced; a few are stars.

When the others discovered his racket, some of them, too, began haunting bus stations. Our enterprising friend again jumped the gun.

He began going to Philadelphia, where he boarded a northbound bus from the deep south. It's 100 miles from Philly to New York. Joe is a fast worker. Before the bus reached Newark, he had the names of all the likely squabs.

O.K. So you're in New York now. If you came by plane, the airline limousine will transport you to the center of the city. Smart guys take a cab from the airport. It's faster, and it's as cheap or cheaper if two or more are riding. But if you arrived by train, you'll face your first major problem trying to get a cab at Grand Central or Pennsylvania Terminal.

(INSIDE STUFF: New York cabs are permitted to carry no more than one party and no more than six passengers.)

Your redcap will be of great assistance, but you must let him know in advance that you'll take care of him liberally if he puts you in a cab.

(The railroad exacts a charge of 25 cents for each unit carried. The redcap doesn't get this. If you want him to get you a cab, promise him at least $1 for two bags.)

You may stand for an hour at the regular station loading platform. In Grand Central, smarties duck upstairs to Vanderbilt Avenue. At Pennsylvania, they go to the unloading platform instead of the loading one, for the same reason.

It is hoped you made your hotel reservation in advance, before leaving home, and got a wire confirming. New York has the worst housing shortage in history and no building program can overcome it before 1955.

But if you are an optimist and didn't make arrangements, don't ask strangers in stations to recommend a hotel or rooming house.

And never take a cab driver's advice.

The Travelers' Aid Society maintains a desk at all

terminals where such information is free. Or else step into a phone booth and call the Hotel Association of New York.

Young people, especially girls, who do not know their way around, are especially invited to make use of the Travelers' Aid facilities. It's no disgrace, no confession of weakness. It's protection. The public supports it.

Girls are warned not to talk to strangers who mosey up to them in stations.

If you know what hotel you're bound for, do not allow the redcap or cab driver to steer you elsewhere.

If the cabbie argues, call a cop, or tell the driver to take you to a police station.

(INSIDE STUFF: Gotham's hack drivers are an honest, intelligent lot, carefully investigated by the police before being given licenses, and seldom involved in crime. A bad one slips in only now and then.)

29. ROOM WITH ADJOINING BLONDE

THERE are "family" hotels in New York, where any woman is your wife. That just goes to show you the variety of accommodations in the Metropolis.

But try to get a room.

It is estimated that Gotham's hostelries can sleep 200,000 guests. But we have a million daily visitors.

When the cab brings you to your hotel, try to look important. We realize that for many that's not easy.

But if you flash big bills while paying the driver and give him a generous tip in view of the doorman, word will precede you before you reach the desk.

(INSIDE STUFF: New York cabbies spit on dime tippers. A quarter is legit, even for a quarter haul.)

You will now stand in front of the awesome functionary known as the room-clerk. Do not quail. Do not quake. Radiate confidence.

If there are no eavesdroppers, try the "I betcha" gag outlined for railroad tickets in the previous chapter.

Say "I betcha 20 bucks you can't give me a room and bath."

But if you think you'll be overheard by others, try this stunt.

Palm a $20 bill in your hand. Reach out to the clerk, shake his flipper and say, "Hi ya, glad to see you again. You've got that reservation for Jones, haven't you?"   *   *   *

For that 20, he will.

In normal times you can be choosey about your hotel, picking the one that suits your tastes and wallet. But now, thank high heaven if you get in a flop joint.

Generally speaking, the kind of yokels we spell with a capital "Y" prefer inns in the Times Square district. The tariffs are moderate and the location ideal for gawkers.

But smart visitors come over to Fifth, Madison, Park and Lexington Avenues. Businessmen quite often check in at hotels near the two rail terminals.

New York's huge needle trade industry is centered around Penn Station. The printing trades cluster around Grand Central.

The chief hotels for women only are the Barbizon, the Allerton and the Martha Washington.* At the Henry Hudson and others there are floors entirely reserved for women. The Y.W.C.A. provides less luxurious but comfortable accommodations.

Invariably, these hotels refuse to permit male visitors in guests' rooms, but in case of illness, physicians are, of course, allowed to visit patients.

Until the management got wise, the favorite ruse of lovelorn couples pleasure bent was for the doll to notify the desk that she was ill and expecting her doctor.

Soon the pseudo-medico would arrive, carrying a black bag. Some gals got away with it . . . but no more. Now, when they say their doctor is coming, the hotel

---

* INSIDE STUFF: If the gal you're calling isn't home, ask the operator at the woman's hotel if any others said they're lonesome. They frequently confide in the "Hello Girl."

nurse remains in the room with the patient all through the "examination."

Most hotels will not rent rooms to ladies and gents who check in without baggage, even though they offer to pay in advance.

* * *

(INSIDE STUFF: But practically every hotel lobby contains a drug or novelty store that sells paper-backed overnight bags, as low as 99 cents. Buy one, fill it with a dozen magazines, and you're set.)

* * *

Hotels, of course, have no legal right to demand to see your wedding license. Suspicious couples are brushed off with the usual, "Sorry, no rooms."

But if you call first, and are given a reservation by phone, then the hotel must accommodate you.

One large and famous New York hostelry was recently stuck for a huge settlement when a perfectly respectable married couple from the suburbs, caught in town over night, phoned for a room.

They were told to come right over. When the room clerk saw no baggage, he refused to permit them to register, though they offered to pay in advance. The irate husband insisted the lady was his wife, but the clerk turned up his nose.

Later, the guests' attorneys proved to the management that it was costly to make such mistakes.

Before the war, many hotels operated OVER-NIGHT CLUBS for their special guests, and by the time this appears in print, may be doing so again.

The privileges of these clubs included the right to check in at any hour of the day or night, with or without your wife, and without questions if you possessed no baggage other than the girl.

In that event, the hotel supplied pajamas, toothbrush, Kleenex, razor blades, etc., as well as feminine requisites, even intimate ones. Among the hotels with Overnight Clubs were the Waldorf, the Lexington, the Piccadilly, Plymouth and some branches of the Knott Chain.

Membership in these clubs was obtained by advance reference that could be checked or by being recommended by other members.

Application to hotel credit managers will enable you to open a charge account at most hotels and have bills sent to your home or office, in or out of town. You can cash checks, too.

* * *

(INSIDE STUFF: It is a specific crime to obtain lodging or food in a hotel with intent to defraud . . . But hotels are obligated by common and statute laws to serve all comers to their capacity . . . Guests may not be barred because of race or creed or the cut of their clothes . . . But hotels are not required to cater to intoxicated or disorderly persons . . . Their Association will spend a fortune to track down anyone who swindles them out of a few dollars.)

* * *

Most New York inns are liberal, adult in their attiture toward visitors of the opposite sex, even at night.

So long as you are quiet and orderly, and don't shout or keep your radio on too loud, the house dick probably won't bother you.

There is even some doubt among legal experts here whether New York hotels have the right to throw customers out into the street for the mere offense of entertaining gals or guys—as the case may be—in their rooms, because they failed to stop off at Niagara Falls.

* * *

(INSIDE STUFF: If you permit someone—even of the same sex—to occupy your room all night, without first registering him or her in at the desk, the hotel can prosecute you for defrauding it of the extra tariff charged for two in a room.)

* * *

In 1945, the house detective of a West Side hotel catering to tourists and the family trade, busted into a room occupied by a female guest—redheaded—because he saw a soldier enter it.

He found the couple in an embarrassing state of negligee.

The gal covered herself as well as she could, told the dick the man she was entertaining was her husband.

"Lady, I've heard that one before," replied the flat-foot.

But here's the pay-off: They *were* married. He was en route through town from one camp to another, had four hours between trains. It was in the afternoon, so she didn't bother to check him in.

Both sued the hotel for fabulous sums. His was thrown out because he wasn't a registered guest. But the courts awarded the gal a heavy judgment.

Hotels are, of course, required by law to provide every possible protection for the property and persons of guests. The innkeeper is not responsible for the loss of portable valuables such as jewels or money, unless checked or in safe-deposit boxes, furnished free on request.

When leaving your room, always double lock the door from the outside. While this precaution will not prevent a sneak thief from entering, it will enable police to determine, from the condition of the lock, whether it was an outside job or an inside one with a passkey.

* * *

Hotel lobbies are convenient places for lonesome people of either sex to find someone to help them forget their loneliness. But if you are NOT looking for adventure DO NOT talk to strangers in lobbies.

It's wise not to mention your room number to strangers whom you meet in lobbies, and don't answer a knock on your room door unless the visitor has first announced himself on the house phone.

Many a gal has been konked on the head and raped, and many a man has found himself knocked out and his valuables gone because they opened to a tap.

* * *

If you hear a disturbance in another room, don't get helpful and join in. Phone the desk, or forget it.

* * *

(INSIDE STUFF: Switchboard operators at most hotels have been instructed by the management to listen in on your calls and report pertinent things they hear.

That's how they get wise, even in the biggest hotels, when you have a visitor in your room, often before the visitor arrives.)

* * *

New York hotels are not set up for kids or dogs. Many will not accept guests with animals. Find out if yours will before bringing the mutt from home.

* * *

A show girl we know recently told us that only dumb girls prefer musicians. She said smart gals chose bartenders and captains of waiters for sweethearts, because these gentry always have money—and while she waited for them to finish work, she could drink champagne—at the boss's expense.

But, said the cutie, the best of all guys—if a twerp is lucky enough to get one—is a hotel bellhop. The only trouble with that aristocracy, she continued, was that they were too snooty and hard to get. They have the pick of the hotel.

The bell captain is the kingpin. He knows everyone

256

and everything, can get you liquor after closing, women, men, anything at any hour; find a pair of nylons, a traveling crap game, or clean diapers for your pride and joy.

Conveniences and necessities provided by this functionary are to be rewarded lavishly. Ask for him if you want extraordinary service.

It is difficult and dangerous to fall in with streetwalkers on the avenues, and next to impossible to locate a gambling den or a house of joy.

But the cops can't put a man on every bellboy. Many of them become intermediaries for purveyors of the particular kind of surreptitious pleasure you may seek; many also use them when the end in view isn't particularly sinful.

For instance, they are strangers in town, find themselves in the mood to see a show or go dancing with a nice young lady. What do they do? Call the boy, of course. He gets them what they want.

There is a difference—more than a subtle difference —between "call" girls and "party" girls, as previously set out.

Those in the first category go through all the earlier motions—and the later ones, too. But the party girls are just what their name implies.

They'll dine and dance with you, court and even romance with you. But they aren't prostitutes, if that's what you're looking for, and when it's time to go home, they go to their own home, unless you've clicked hard and registered high appeal.

Many of these gals are models or show gals trying to earn a few extra bucks, honestly.

Some of the call girls are also models or chorines, but their extra few bucks aren't earned so honestly, by pious standards.

30. TIPS ON THE TOWN

    I. How to duck your wife or husband.
   II. What to do and where to go.
  III. Do it with what?

*　*　*

PROBLEM I is only for the married.

This chapter is mainly concerned with problem II.

As for problem III, you will have to find the where-withal yourself. Those without it are advised to remain in Steubenville and learn about New York from these pages.

Those without wives, husbands, children, mistresses, dogs or other encumbrances may skip the next few paragraphs.

I

Most married men of our acquaintance who visit New York regularly tell their wives it's a business trip and get away with leaving the madame home. Once a year, however, or maybe twice, she insists on coming to Manhattan. She wants to shop and see the shows.

Now, if you are a smart guy, you will try to arrange your next such trip to coincide with the similar hop by your best friend and his wife.

You will find that, if supplied with dough, the women will keep occupied all day every day, foraging in the shops.

Though it's more difficult to get rid of them at night,

259

it can be done if you and your pal are halfway intelligent. You will want to load them up with tickets for all the highbrow shows, the opera and concerts, and pull the oldie about "Hon, you know I'll fall asleep if I sit through that."

Or you can tell 'em you and the pal have an important business date and will meet them at the hotel later.

But if you are here with your old lady and have no one to park her with, you are in trouble.

You can find some free daylight time, naturally, by bundling her off to the shops or the hairdresser's, or alibiing with business. But, we ask you, what are you going to do with yourself in the daytime?

New York is strictly an owl town.

You might take a dance lesson at one of the numerous Arthur Murray branches or sit in a lobby and try your luck at ogling the dolls or kibitz with the manicurist, but none of these are exciting and they can be done better in your home town.

You know your wife better than we do, but if you can't check her in a theatre by herself at night, or if you have no relatives in town to leave her with, you are out of luck.

* * *

Married ladies will not need our professional advice on ducking husbands. They know how. And husbands rarely refuse.

For the married couples who do want to make our town together, but are handicapped by children, dogs

or canaries, ask the bellboy for services that mind in-
fants, walk dogs and sit up with older children.

* * *

MIDNIGHT MANNERS: Don't bring children to
night clubs unless it's someone else's precocious daughter. Visitors, who have no other place to leave them,
are the worst offenders. Caberets are not for schoolkids
—even at the early dinner shows.

II

If you haven't a date, get one.

Call the bellboy or refer to Chapter 33 for friendship services.

* * *

(INSIDE STUFF: When a guy calls for you in a
limousine or private car bearing a license number in
the 82 series, it's rented.

Hirers of rented limousines may be phonies or wise
guys. If you want to make believe, there's no better
way of putting on the dog than engaging a Carey Car—
a brand new Cadillac limousine with uniformed chauffeur, rate $5 an hour, less over considerable periods.

Many legitimate people also use these rented cars,
sometimes hiring them by the month or year. They get
24-hour chauffeur service, perfectly conditioned cars,
and thus eliminate garage, repair and insurance wor-
ries.

Other wise guys use these cars to go to the theatre,
airport or outside the city limits. The fee is only

slightly more than a cab, and cars are always available by phone. It saves time and trouble of waiting and whistling for cabs and arguing with drivers.)

* * *

New York, unlike other large cities, does not permit doubling of parties in taxis, and neither the passenger nor the driver is permitted to make an exception.

Main reason for this rule is Gotham's huge transient population. Permitting strangers to share cabs would open an easy avenue of access for thieves and trollops to meet and make up to their quarry.

Under our law, a cab must take you wherever you want to go inside the city limits.

If the driver refuses to carry you to your destination order him to take you to the nearest police station.

There are no extra charges on or off the meter, other than 50 cents for trunks and waiting time. Pay only what appears on the meter, plus a tip.

* * *

If you are waiting for a cab at a public place, such as a hotel, theatre, night club, railroad station or hack stand, you must take the first in the feed line, if there is one there, instead of grabbing the one discharging passengers. This is a city ordinance.

* * *

It is next to impossible to obtain theatre tickets for the hits, and those you can get you won't want.

* * *

There are, of course, the licensed ticket agents or "brokers" which you will find in every hotel lobby and around Times Square. They are permitted by law to charge a nominal premium.

But these brokers seldom have up-front seats for hits for the same night.

For any sell-out show or for an important baseball, football or other sports event, you must figure in an added premium of from two to five dollars per ticket, often more.

Your bellboy may be able to dig the ducats for you, or he can recommend a scalper who bootlegs them above legal price.

Otherwise, try your luck bribing the ticket agent's clerk.

If you don't have to plan in advance, a good tip is to go to the box office just at curtain time. Quite often you can get excellent seats at list price, and sometimes even cheaper when the last-minute returns come in from the agencies.

The choice tickets for the hits are in the hands of brokers and scalpers long before the shows first come to Broadway, through what is known in theatrical parlance as "buys." The big agencies underwrite the shows before they are produced by buying anywhere from $10,000 to $50,000 worth of tickets in advance.

Many expensive shows could not be produced if this money were not forthcoming from the speculators.

At the same time, the specs take a terrific gamble, for if the show is a flop they are stuck with worthless pasteboard.

That is why the premium for the hits is so steep, to let them recoup losses.

As aforementioned, the licensed officers do not sell tickets to strangers above legal maximums. For that reason, strangers rate only the secondary choice of seats, if any.

The good ones, way down in front, are held back for regular charge customers, for clubs and for the guy who tips the bellboy liberally.

* * *

Restaurant and supper club reservations can be made in advance by phone, but unless the headwaiter knows you, you will find your table behind a post or along the wall when you get there. Also, places like El Morocco refuse phone reservations from all except regulars, and the regulars don't need them.

If you point to one unoccupied in a position of better vantage, the functionary will show you the "Reserved" sign.

The odds are it is not reserved, but is being kept for a liberal tipper.

Now, there are only two ways of beating this system. The first and best is to slip the headwaiter a few bucks. He will suddenly discover that he has made a slight error and the table he is really holding for you is way up front, on the ringside, because the reservee died a few minutes ago.

The other way is to get tough about it and threaten to walk out if he doesn't give you a better table.

If the place is doing any kind of business at all, they

will let you walk. But if they give you a better table it usually shows that things are so bad (either because of a bum show or lousy food) you won't want to stay anyway.

Headwaiters at some of the swank night clubs like the Stork or El Morocco, where most people aren't permitted in unless known, or at busy places like the Copacabana, are reputed to make more than the owners.

Some estimate that $5,000 a week for these factotums is conservative. They may have to kick some back. They all pay for their jobs instead of being paid for them.

(INSIDE STUFF about theatre tickets:

Though most houses invariably number their seats as A1, B2, and so on, there are exceptions.

Ticket C1, for example, is not always first seat on the aisle, third row.)

See page 299 for a list of theatres where the numbering system varies from the norm.

The reveler who plans to visit a café or supper club will find that a knowledge of the name of the headwaiter, maître d'hôtel or proprietor of the place quite often helps obtain a better table or service.

See page 301 for a directory of such functionaries at New York's leading spots.

New York has more taxis per capita than any other city anywhere, but even in normal times, when the full quota of 20,000 is on the streets, it's difficult to get them at certain times.

Few New Yorkers use their own cars to come to the

shopping or theatre centers of town, because of the traffic and parking problems. Cab fares are so cheap and distances so short in Manhattan that few people are too poor to use cabs.

Most difficult times of day to get taxis are between 5 and 6, at the close of business hours; 8 o'clock at the theatre rush; 11 P.M., when the plays let out; and 4 A.M., when the night clubs close.

At night you can tell if a taxi is vacant. The light over the driver's compartment is then shining. In the daytime, watch the flag on his meter. If it's up, he's free.

(INSIDE STUFF: If you have trouble flagging a cab at 8 P.M., it's because the driver doesn't want to take calls into the theatre district, where the fare comes to but a few cents. He gets stuck without a return load.)

So, if you're not going to a Times Square show, shout that fact to a cabbie. Maybe he'll stop if he hears you.

Better still, stand on a one-way street bound *away* from Broadway, and indicate with your thumb that you're bound opposite from the White Way.

* * *

Contrary to general belief, New York is not an overly "dressy" town.

In many midwest metropolises people "dress" more at night than they do here, but certainly without as much success.

Even in the very best places, patronized by the bluest

of the bloods, you will always see more men and women informal than in soup and fish.

New Yorkers generally dress only when the occasion demands it, such as the opera, an important theatrical opening, or a formal affair.

(INSIDE STUFF: The "tuxedo" or dinner jacket is semi-formal, not formal. When good dressers wear it, they wear turndown, never wing, collars.)

But if New Yorkers do not dress formally every time they go out, they surely dress with taste.

New York women seldom wear hats.

They NEVER wear white or pastels in the summer, nor white shoes or stockings.

Black is proper all year, even during the dog days.

Best-dressed men always wear hats, never wear sport clothes in the city.

* * *

MIDNIGHT MANNERS:

Wise dolls never wear two different kinds of flowers with one ensemble. If the chump sends you orchids, chuck the fake roses out of your hair.

It may be warm, but babe, if your construction calls for a girdle, wear it, at least while dancing.

During the rainy spring season and the slushy winter, do not dance with your galoshes on. Not that we care how funny you look, but it ruins the polish on the floor.

267

Women who wear evening gowns with cut-out backs should hide their straps and bras. (Women who need bras should not wear evening gowns with cut-out backs.)

The best dressed dolls never wear corsages in our town, but clucks insist on sending them. If you must, white orchids go with anything, but they cost $15 a throw. You may ask the lady what she is wearing and be guided accordingly. All orchids are in good taste; camellias and gardenias are cheaper but according to Hoyle, and violets are okay for afternoons. But well-dressed dolls never wear roses, lilies of the valley or such garden truck.

Dames with turret tummies should not wear evening gowns with bare midriffs.

This is one we thought we'd never have to mention: Dames who cover evening gowns with street coats look ludicrous.

(INSIDE STUFF: When you spot a New York gal in the subway so attired, ten to one she's a taxi-dancer en route to work at the hall, dressed for the evening's labor. Odds are 100 to 1 if she's also carrying a make-up case.)

Gents never wear brown shoes or tweeds after 6 P.M.

It is crude for femmes to wear wrist watches with evening gowns. (If you've got to know the time, look into your boy friend's eyes.)

Dolls who wear tight dresses shouldn't eat until they bust. If you have to open the zipper at the side of your dress or pop out at the seam, cut down on the intake, honey. You can load up again when you get back into the house dress, on the farm.

No smart filly rolls her stockings. (Garter belts are a must—or don't wear hose.) For, when she's dancing and her skirt swishes around her knees, the bulge breaks the symmetry of the limb. Nylon all the way up is sexier and smarter.

31. INSIDE STUFF

FLIRTING: Don't. If you do on the street, you're apt to be arrested, and in the subway, killed.

MARRIAGE: Licenses are issued and ceremonies performed at City Hall, and in the Borough Halls of the outlying boroughs. A Wassermann test is necessary for bride and bridegroom and 72 hours must elapse between issuance of license and the fatal words. The nearest state where marriages are performed without delay is South Carolina.

DIVORCE: There is only one ground for divorce in New York State: Adultery, proven by two eye-witnesses. A few uncontested divorces are finagled by collusion between husband and wife, the former allowing himself to be raided while with a paid corespondent. There are no residence requirements for divorce. Final papers are issued after 90 days. The guilty party in an adultery action (obtained anywhere) cannot remarry in the state without permission of a Supreme Court Justice. Most New Yorkers remarry in New Jersey. New York courts have ruled these marriages valid.

CLIP JOINTS: To be avoided, unless you are looking for grief. These deadfalls, usually in old brownstone houses on side streets, in Greenwich Village or Harlem, operate without licenses. The sucker is steered by a runner or cab driver who promises "women." Bills are brutally padded, bank checks raised, drinks loaded with knockout drops. If you protest, you'll have your hair parted with a bottle.

CURFEW CATCH: We're going to give you a hot tip. Don't say we told you, but if you have an unfinished drink (or even bottle) on your table at 4 A.M., neither the club nor the cops can make you scram until you've finished it. The law here does not require liquor be removed on the stroke of curfew—merely that the bar close, the music and entertainment cease. See you at 4:01.

Though the legal closing is 4 A.M. daily, bars are required to shutter at 3 o'clock Saturday nights only (of all times). But clubs may sell food and entertainment until 4. What we noted about it being kosher to keep liquor on your table after the curfew, week nights, also goes for Sunday morn. Anything served before 3 may be consumed during the next hour, even after, if the weary waiters don't thumb you on your way.

AFTER-HOUR SPOTS AND BOTTLE CLUBS: These used to be common, but few New Yorkers now seem willing or able to imbibe after the deadline. There remain practically no too-late spots. The few that do, pose as private clubs, selling no liquor, but serving "members" out of their own lockers. (If they know you well, your locker, by coincidence, is always stocked with just your brand.) Celebs go to the Club Carr, on Fifth Avenue, at E. 69th St. Once raided, not for liquor, but for entertainment sans license, the club beat the rap. Another is the Gold Key, W. 56th near Sixth Avenue.

CABARET INFO: Hostesses are not permitted in

clubs. Female entertainers are forbidden to sit out with customers. Waitresses may not be employed after midnight, except in hotels.

Most night clubs present the first show at 8 or 8:30, their second at 12 or 12:30 and their last at 2 or 2:30.

The Latin Quarter presents two shows nightly, except on Saturday, three.

Few clubs except the Stork and El Morocco have a cover charge. But most good hotel grill rooms do.

All other clubs have minimum charges, from $2 to $5 on weekdays, up to $6 a person at some, Saturdays and $7.50 opening nights.

Though it's not a law, the cops have advised saloon-keepers they don't like 'em to cater to unescorted ladies after 10 P.M. even if they come in groups, so you femmes sans boy friends had better get yourselves one if you want to see our night life.

TIPS: If you want to get into many night clubs, or get good tables in any, you have to stake the head-waiter, the tip ranging from $2 in the more modest places up to $10 and $20 at the Stork and El Morocco.

Waiters, too, expect more here than in other cities. A 10 per cent tip will earn you an icy stare most anywhere. The average night club habitué usually adds on about 25 per cent, but more often figures the tip on the length of time he occupied the table and the amount of service he received. In other words, if his check was only $2, but he sat at the table so long the waiter lost two or three other parties, he'd reward him accordingly.

WAITERS' RACKETS: Padded checks and switched

checks are common. In the first instance, the waiter makes a "mistake" in the addition, in his favor, then, after you pay, he erases the wrong total and turns in the correct amount. On the switch racket, he presents you with a larger check written for another table. Most people don't study the items. But if you do, he apologizes and says he gave you the wrong check. If you pay, he turns in your smaller right check, pockets the difference, then uses the large check over again.

CHECK YOUR HAT: Your "voluntary" contribution to the hat-room gal isn't as voluntary as you imagine. The concessionaire's license from the city permits him to exact a flat charge for each item checked, if he desires.

Hat-check and cigarette girls turn in all their tips (except those they manage secretly to pocket). They are paid $30 or $35 a week and a percentage of tips over $1. Camera girls are permitted to keep their tips, turning the $1.50 per picture over to the concessionaire, who splits with the cabaret.

The larger concessionaires have become the bankers of the night club business. Without them, half the town's clubs would not have been able to open in the first place. Some of the larger clubs reap up to $50,000 a year for the privilege of checking your kellys. This money is paid in advance to new clubs, often covering construction costs. The concessionaire takes a mortgage on the enterprise to protect his investment. When a club goes broke, the concessionaire finds himself in possession of it. To keep his girls working, he turns it over to another operator, advances more money, takes more mortgage.

I CAN GET IT FOR YOU WHOLESALE: You'd be surprised how many guys make a living buying things for their friends "strictly at cost." This is the town where every inhabitant thinks he's a wise gee and squarely on the inside.

So he figures that retail stores are strictly for chumps, strangers, and the other fellow.

At the same time, practically everyone in New York either has a relative or knows someone with a relative who works in a wholesale house.

When his friend, or even his relative, takes him to the showroom, he's convinced he's being let in on the ground floor. Prices in wholesale establishments are never marked on the ticket.

So the wholesaler always jacks on a tidy sum, enough to take care of the steerer and give himself a neat profit (which he doesn't enter on the books and so doesn't pay tax on).

And the wise chump goes out, happy and feeling privileged, whereas he probably paid more than if he had shopped over the counter at a reputable store.

HOW TO BEAT THE HORSES: Some smart Gotham gazelles have worked out a sure-fire way to get a stake.

Whereas most guys won't be touted by men, they don't look at it that way when a cute filly (homo sapiens, not equine) asks them to put a bet on a certain horse for her.

Now, if she knows enough chumps and can get bets

down on the three leading horses in any one race, it's practically positive she's going to collect on one.

And no gent is going to ask the cutie to pay up for losers. (We don't recommend this unless the gams look nice in nylon.)

THE "PRODUCERS": All these guys produce is a bank roll for themselves. They're usually good-looking middle-aged fellows who dance and drink well, sling clever small talk and know everyone.

Their stock is their ability to flatter wealthy old dames and procure phone numbers of pert young patooties for wealthy old codgers.

When working on an overaged, rich hag who may be a widow or married to a guy who is happy to find a companion for his ugly wife so he can go stepping too, the "producer" gives out with the woo and ends up with a "backer" for the show he intends to produce, but never gets around to. The initial overhead, meaning himself, always eats up the bank roll.

On the other hand, if his backer is a rutty old male, the approach is to get him a girl, then sell the idea that she should be starred.

These "producers" live well, often luxuriously, dance and dine at the best and make Palm Beach every winter.

But we don't call them gigolos or pimps, because the former work for five dollars an hour and the latter live off five-buck bims. This is big business.

THE INTRODUCERS: Hundreds of smart New York articles live and thrive because they manage to know the right people and can introduce you to whomever you want to know—banker, politico, social leader —on 15 minutes' notice.

They travel in the best circles, are smooth, suave and likeable. For the proper fee, they'll provide connections with senators, governors or financiers.

After that, it's up to you.

SHARKS: Don't carry large sums of money with you and don't flash it; don't carry your billfold in your hip pocket; don't give money to touts who promise a "sure thing"; don't play cards or shoot craps with strangers.

RETIRING ROOM: We were in Sherm Billingsley's Stork with a curious young lady from Boston, who wanted to know why our washroom was on the main floor, whereas she had to climb a flight. That's simple. Young men don't patronize expensive clubs, so who could expect vets like us or Charlie Chaplin or George Jessel or George Jean Nathan to climb stairs? Whereas the filly is young, healthy and husky.

MUZHIKS—How to Spot One: He has a round haircut, a short coat, with or without belt in back, sleeves pressed into a razor-blade crease, carries shiny fountain pens and pencils in the kerchief pocket of his jacket, wears a lodge pin and a vest (which usually doesn't meet his trousers).

32. MIDNIGHT MANNERS

GENEROUSLY BUILT dames should not sit on backless bar stools. Did you ever stand behind one? Did you ever see an Alp?

* * *

When night clubbing, keep your paw off your lady friend's leg. There's a time and place for everything.

* * *

Eating habits and appetites are personal. We snipers should keep our snoots out. But if you are a greenie in Gotham, trying to impress the headwaiter or Follies dollies with sophistication, DO NOT drink your coffee with your meal. Wait until AFTER dessert. DO NOT eat your salad as an appetizer (à la Hollywood) or as a side-dish (à la Chicago). Only between roast and dessert. This is New York.

* * *

Any man who wears white or two-toned shoes for dancing at any place above a coffee-pot should be sentenced to walk back in them to his farm.

* * *

Gents who like to dance cheek-to-cheek, say the dolls, should be closely shaven. But one who dances cheek-to-cheek ain't no gent!

Do not table-hop in clubs. Never go to strange tables and ask women you do not know to dance. You may get a smack on the kisser. But, if you don't, you may be bounced out. It is against the law for night clubs to permit people to mix from table to table. Besides, it's corny, which is worse than illegal.

* * *

Gals should not straighten the seams of their stockings in the middle of the dance-floor. There are easier ways to attract attention to the gams.

* * *

When entering a night club, don't head for the powder-room before the captain has shown you to your table, otherwise your escort has to stand in the crowded lobby waiting for you and looking foolish (while you take the usual 45 minutes!).

* * *

When the lady says she has to go, it is customary to give her four bits for the pro in the powder-room. Which reminds us of the tale about the gal whose nose got shiny eight or ten times, night after night, at great cost to her John. After five years, she walked out on him and bought an apartment house in the Bronx.

Warning: Most night clubs have phone booths in the ladies' room. That's where they call the guy they meet after they brush you off.

* * *

Weaklings who tend to become absent-minded after the third drink are advised to place their hat check in the upper left breast pocket. One blotto bird in a narrow night club foyer, yelling for his coat and insisting he never got a check, can hold up 300. When the checker assists the customer she is instructed to begin looking for the ducat in that pocket, working down and back therefrom.

* * *

The reverse table-hopper is as bad a pest as the original. Don't demand the acquaintances at the next table join your party. Maybe they want to be alone!

* * *

Don't stare!

* * *

Don't try to get too hot with a girl in public, or you'll wind up with the cold shoulder. If you want to hold hands, do it under the table. That's what long tablecloths are for. Don't try to hog the dance-floor, unless you want to be a pig shot. While an entertainer is working, don't turn around and tell your friends what a great pal of yours he or she is—loud enough to drown him or her out.

* * *

Dolls who understandably want to show off their fur coats in cabarets should think of a better method than to drape them over the back of the chair and onto the floor, where they become traffic hazards for passing waiters and guests. Dames who do this deserve skunk, not mink.

* * *

Dames too ample in certain regions should not wear tight skirts for dancing. (Watch the next one and see what we mean.)

* * *

When a lady stops to chat at a table where men are present, she should ask the men to keep their chairs or she should sit down, so the guys won't be kept standing while she gabbles. If she does neither, she's no lady, and no man need then bother.

* * *

When a lunkhead and his twist spat in a night club, it's etiquette for him to dash after her and slip her cab fare.

* * *

Dolls who must cross their pins at ringside tables should be sure they have nice ones.

* * *

When the emcee announces that the chorines will go through the room to collect for the Red Cross, don't suddenly decide to phone.

* * *

If you have to go—or if you're coming back—while an entertainer is working, don't cross the dance-floor in front of the artist. Wait until the number is over; or, if you can, circumnavigate—flank the performer.

* * *

While dancing, don't wave to a friend at a table. You may put someone's eye out . . . If your shoelace opens, don't stop on the dance-floor to tie it—move off.

* * *

If you must take somebody's phone number, write it at your table, not while on the floor. (Don't take it at all if her brute is bigger than you.)

* * *

Do not show off on dance-floors. Even if you are as hep as Fred Astaire, the other customers do not want to see you. Besides, the bouncer is not sympathetic to amateur talent.

* * *

The almost morbid desire of young women to look in mirrors brings on one of the most horrendous of all night club gaucheries . . . when the sweet young things duck from their escorts every half-hour and remain away for time without limit while the escorts squirm alone. The condition is doubly disastrous when two or more young women are in the party, because whenever one goes, all go, and they stay forever while they discuss the men, who know it.

* * *

If the poetry in your soul forces you to beat time to singing or music, use your fingers, not a tablespoon.

* * *

It's atrocious taste for two females to dance together. Good spots won't permit it, though some of the clap-trap caravansaries catering to tourists or sewing-circle society parties stand for it until 10.

* * *

If your escort asks you to dance, don't turn him down. If you're tired, don't make dates. But if he doesn't want to dance, DON'T BE A PEST AND BEG.

* * *

When you see a friend with a squab in a cabaret, don't suggest that you and your pigeon move to his table and make it a foursome. He may have IMPOR-TANT business to discuss.

* * *

If somebody else's dish (and we mean dish, not doll) looks particularly attractive, don't sample it unless you're first asked to. If you'd like to try it, order from the waiter!

* * *

Do not eat garlic or onions unless your escort also does. (Or unless you want to keep the wolf from your door.)

* * *

We've already inveighed against the bore who table-hops and asks to dance with your dame. Now the might of our wrath is directed toward the gal who makes things worse for her man by encouraging the intruder. When a stranger comes to your table, say "No," immediately. Don't prolong the agony by turning to your escort and asking if you should dance with the drunk or dope.

33. CONFIDENTIAL GUIDE TO NEW YORK

AMUSEMENT PARKS: Back-breaking sky-rides, pink lemonade, cotton candy and hot dogs are available at Coney Island's famed Steeplechase (BMT subway); Palisades Park in Fort Lee, N. J. Bring your own gal or pick one up.

* * *

ASTROLOGERS AND FORTUNE TELLERS: Predicting futures is against the law, but horoscope readings are not. (Consult Classified phone directory for "Astrologers.") Many night clubs employ "readers" who "analyze your palm, handwriting or tea leaves." Service is gratis, but you're expected to shell at least a buck.

Inside Stuff: Society babes have their palms read at the Golden Earring—54th and Madison.

Midnight Manners: When your gal is having her fortune told by the night club palmist, don't listen in. The seer will say a tall, dark man is coming into her life. And you're probably short, fat and gray.

Wisdom of a White Way Wolf: Slip the palmist a fin before she starts. A short, fat and gray man will plunge into the gal's life.

* * *

BABY SITTERS: Phone SU 7-6779. If she's over 15 call us.

* * *

BALLET: Personally, it's way above us. We don't like muscular calves. But the longhairs say we have some of the best ballet in the world. Consult daily papers.

* * *

BARBER SHOPS, LATE: If you get an unexpected night call, and you haven't a razor blade, you're out of luck. There aren't any all-night barber shops any more, since two gorillas were killed in one. Most of them close at 8; in Grand Central and Penn Terminals, at 9. The following shops are open until midnight: Victoria, West 51st Street; Taft Hotel; Spinrad's, 50th and Broadway; Dawn Patrol, Seventh Avenue and 53rd Street; Claridge Hotel. (All cabaret men's room attendants will supply safety razors and blades.) Barber shops are closed Sundays, except in private clubs.

* * *

BOATING: Row boats are available in all the city parks in summer, at two bits an hour (peanuts for yourself and the ducks, extra). Swell way to woo a doll; she can't walk home.

* * *

BRIDGE GAMES FOUND: Are you looking for congenial opponents? Call Mildred Lovejoy, CO 5-

9290. Or try the bridge clubs in many hotels. Though patrons are charged for playing, the law says they aren't gambling houses. Why? We wouldn't know. For lessons, Banfield, PL 5-0980, or Cummings, CO 5-9515.

* * *

BURLESQUE: Who brought that up?

* * *

BUS RIDES: Hurry, hurry, hurry, if you still want New York's cheapest thrill, riding with your gal on top of a Fifth Avenue bus. The company is gradually retiring all the double deckers. No open-top buses are left, anyway.

* * *

CHAPERON SERVICE (For girls or unaccompanied wives): If pretty, call us.

* * *

CLEANERS, ONE DAY: Yep, we still have 'em here. Your hotel valet will take care of it; otherwise Misch, on West 47th Street.

Midnight Manners: Don't smear your lipstick on a man's lapel while dancing. Cleaning rouge and powder stains is expensive. And his wife might get fussy.

* * *

CLOTHES REWOVEN: If the doll accidentally burns your suit instead of you, while protecting herself with her cigarette from your mad advances, consult the Classified phone directory.

286

Wisdom of a White Way Wolf: You should wait until she finishes the cigarette.

* * *

COMFORT STATIONS AND REST ROOMS: Saloonkeepers aren't hospitable to men's room cus--tomers and get downright sore at ladies' room patrons. But if you gotta, all subway stations have free comfort stations, usually filthy. Often degenerates and thugs lurk there. Many hotels maintain pay (5 or 10 cents) stations, others have the tip-as-you-go system. Minimum, 25 cents, if you use a towel. Rest rooms in railroad stations are open all night. (Fee, 5 and 10 cents. Also baths, 25 cents and up.) Free comfort stations, operated by the city at 47th Street and Broadway, 60th and Central Park West, 42nd Street behind the library, and in all parks.

* * *

CONCERTS: You'd be surprised how many young chippies patronize Carnegie Hall since Stokowski took Gloria Vanderbilt away from Pat di Cicco. Our chief concert and recital halls are Carnegie Hall, Town Hall, Steinway Hall, and Times Hall, with the City Center Theatre often going in for same.

* * *

CONFIDENTIAL DETECTIVES: Bolan (ex-Commissioner of Police) Agency, Empire State Building, LA 4-5100.

* * *

DANCING: Smart guys find too much dancing interferes with romancing. It saps the gal's energy and their own; sobers her up if she's had a few; makes her miss the drinks she'd consume if she were sitting at the table. But, if you'd rather dance than progress, New York's the place for it. Almost all its 1,500 cabarets present dance music; there are dozens of dance halls where you can go; and the Y's, churches and other social organizations throw hops on the slightest provocation. But, unlike smaller towns, there's neither cocktail nor lunch dancing here. (Revolting thought—dancing at lunch time.)

But dinner and supper dancing: How can you miss it?

If you haven't a partner, any dance hall will supply you one at a small fee per dance. Or you can easily pick one up, as unescorted ladies are permitted in all the halls, usually at a reduced fee to encourage attendance.

If you can't dance, you will find hundreds of studios in the Classified directory, guaranteeing to teach you in from five to ten lessons.

You will find some of these studios (especially a number in old brownstone houses on the West Side) sell more than dancing instructions. It's up to you to feel your way.

If you're a swing addict, consult the newspaper ads for the places where that kind of band is playing, usually at a hotel grill.

Club bands play mostly rumbas and sambas, with a few fox trots and hardly any waltzes except at the dreamy hour, after 3 A.M.

New Yorkers are not jitterbugs. Most clubs hustle jive addicts off the floor.

TERP TIPS: You dames with wide circumferences should not rumba. If you must, please don't quake below the equator.

Don't shift your right hand up and down her spine while dancing, like a chiropractor or indecisive sax player . . . Don't be a floor hog . . . Don't grab the girl around the waist, hiking her dress up by inches. (Why not? That's why we sit at ringsides.)

Don't ask the band leader to play a conga unless you want to be spotted as a square-head.

When the band plays a rumba or samba, if you can't do it, remain at your table instead of trying to dance a fox trot to the complicated rhythm. New York is the only city where a large part of the dance program consists of rumbas and sambas. (In the East Side clubs they form the major part.)

Never chew gum when dancing—but if you must, do it in time to the music!

Most clubs feature two bands with continuous music, whereas small-town cabarets operate with one, which usually plays a set of three tunes, then 10-minute intermissions. So it is suggested that when you ask a gal for a dance in a New York club, you release her from your clinging embrace after a maximum of 15 minutes. Though the music goes on forever, the endurance doesn't.

* * *

DRUGSTORES, ALL NIGHT: Lexington and

49th; 66th and Columbus; Seventh and 52nd Street; Seventh and 51st; Broadway and 50th; 47th and Broadway; Seventh and 50th; Broadway and 44th.

* * *

EMERGENCY INFO: Birth Control Ass'n, 220 East 12th Street, AL 4-4437; Birth Control Bureau for Marriage Consultation, 55 East 86th Street, AT 9-4250; Birth Control Center, IWO, 80 Fifth Avenue, AL 4-2321; Margaret Sanger Research Bureau, WA 9-6200; Planned Parenthood Federation, WI 2-8600.

* * *

ERRANDS: To pick up railroad tickets, send flowers, call for your laundry or get your lunch, phone Rapid, EL 5-6100; Mercury, LE 2-0543; Airline, VA 6-5145; Western Union, WO 2-7111.

* * *

ESCHATOLOGIST: Oh, yes. We have one of those, too. Whatever it is. Mrs. M. E. Nase, Lorraine 2-8722.

* * *

ESCORTS: At Your Service, MU 9-4378—Hostesses, too.

* * *

FRIENDS—TO MEET NEW ONES: Personally we're misanthropes, but if you're lonely and haven't the guts to brave strangers, phone ABC, WI 7-2430; Social, TR 3-2013, or Clara Lane, LU 2-2617.

* * *

GIRDLES—FIRST AID: If your favorite girdle busts while you're away from home, call Jean Kaufman, 54 West 56th Street. But if you're the kind who needs a girdle, why didn't you stay home?

* * *

GAMBLING: All forms, except on-track pari-mutuel, are illegal, but you will have little trouble finding bookmakers and policy-slip sellers. There are no casinos or gambling houses as such in the city limits. As soon as one gets started, the cops crack down. There are no exceptions. Yet you can find card games going in some political clubs and so-called social and bridge clubs. Traveling crap games are common around Broadway and in Harlem, and there are steerers to take you to them.

Slot machines are vigorously banned, but of late the authorities have been winking at a new type of electrical gambling machine, similar to pinball, which pays off on poker hands. These are being set up in some of the best midtown locations and in other parts of town, and though they pay off in "merchandise," which is as illegal as cash, they seem to have plenty of protection way up. Some buy back the "merchandise" for currency. Frank Costello makes them.

* * *

HORSE RACING: You can lose your money pleasantly at Belmont, Aqueduct, Empire and Jamaica, all within the city limits or environs. Betting is by pari-mutuel, with bookmaking and off-track betting forbidden. But how are you going to put a fly cop in every cigar store, saloon, newstand, elevator, lobby and bellboy's cap?

* * *

LOTTERIES AND NUMBERS: It's agin the law, as your soda jerk or cigar clerk tells you, as he sells you.

* * *

MAID SERVICE: in your apartment, by day, week or month. Also housemen, wall and window washers, baby sitters. Bennett, SP 7-7820; Maid-to-Order, TR 3-3185; Taylor-Maid, TE 8-7171.

* * *

MANICURISTS: All barber shops and hotels. Some want their nails filed, others just like to sit and talk to the cute ones. But why is it any different here than in your own home town, where lonesome bucks always go first for the finger mechanics?

* * *

MASSEURS: Some people go to masseurs to be massaged and some masseurs massage, but some use the title to cover an older going-over. Sorry, you'll have to find them yourself. We don't ache enough for a massage.

* * *

MIDWIFES: If you're in that condition, don't come to New York. If you do come, get a doctor. But if you're old-fashioned and demand a midwife, you'll find some in the Classified phone directory.

* * *

PALMISTS: They're against the law, but Diana, LO 5-4530 is a "hand analyst."

* * *

PARTIES PLANNED: We like our parties impromptu, you know, like when the blonde drops in unexpectedly and says: "Let's get stinko." But if you like to entertain and want to do it big, call Service Delicatessen, BU 8-7384; Daniel, PL 9-5941; for children's parties, Arnold. Amusements and entertainment provided, Harrington, CI 6-5979.

* * *

RENT, FOR: You can rent practically anything in New York, including a wife, but not an apartment. If you are interested in hiring any of the following, consult the Classified phone directory: Airplanes, bikes, cameras, cars, diamonds, evening clothes, furs, private railroad cars, radios, typewriters and yachts. (No open listing for wives.)

* * *

SHOOTING GALLERIES: What's the matter, bud, didn't you have enough of it in the Army? If not, try Broadway and 48th Street, Broadway and 51st Street, or Sixth Avenue between 42nd and 47th; 42nd

Street between Broadway and Eighth Avenue, or any amusement park.

* * *

SHOPPING SERVICES: Will buy anything for you from a layette to a tombstone, except a broad or bride. At Your Service, MU 9-4370; Lili Personal Service, MU 2-5266; Finders, MU 2-8196.

* * *

SHOW GALS: Consult newspaper for current musical attractions. Or visit these night clubs: Latin Quarter, Copacabana, Leon & Eddie's, Hotel New Yorker (on ice skates). Rockettes at Radio City Music Hall and Gae Foster girls at the Roxy.

* * *

SIGHT-SEEING: The rubberneck buses are back. You'll find steerers at every Times Square corner.

* * *

SKY VIEWS: Surest way to wow a wench is to take her to the 102nd floor observatory of Empire State Building on a clear, starlit night. The thrilling view of the city below, twinkling lights that look like diamonds on a giant diadem, will bring something into her eyes. If you need help, there's an excellent cocktail bar in the observatory, highest on earth. Other observatories, RCA, Chrysler and Woolworth Buildings.

* * *

SWIMMING: Why pay a premium for a front row ticket at a musical when you can see more at any beach? New York's popular public beaches are not recommended, as the waters are unsanitary, crowded and dirty. Those with dough belong to clubs in Long Island or Jersey, where water is clean and girls ditto. Smart ones, without much money, patronize pools.

* * *

TELEGRAPH OFFICE—ALL NIGHT: If you have to wire home for money after an evening: Western Union, at 40th and Broadway, Penn Station and Grand Central, always open. Or phone WO 2-7111.

* * *

WAKE UP SERVICE: If you can't get up after that big night with the blonde, phone MU 7-6500. But who's going to wake you first?

* * *

WALL STREET AND STOCK MARKET: Talking of gambling, a few pages back, how about it? But even if you're not a gambler, an ogle at the greatest money mart is a daytime kick. But the Stock and Curb Exchanges are closed to visitors. You can look at Trinity Church, though.

* * *

WET NURSES: Who thought of that one? Phone New York Academy of Medicine, AT 9-4700, and ask for "Information."

WORRIER, PROFESSIONAL: You may not have had a care in the world when you picked up this volume. But now you rate a nervous breakdown. Under the heading "Psychologists" in the Classified directory, you will find guys willing to do your worrying—for a fee, of course. They advise on sex and the lack of it. If you get any good info, please advise the authors. (For inclusion in the next edition, of course.)

PART FOUR

THE APPENDIX
(*Confidential!*)

A. BACKSTAGE PHONE NUMBERS

THEATRES

	Back Stage No.
'Adelphi	CI 5-9298
Alvin	CO 5-8709
Belasco	JU 6-9570
Bijou	CI 5-9731
Booth	CH 4-9677
Broadhurst	CH 4-9145
Carnegie Hall	CI 7-1350
Center Theatre	CI 5-9590
Century	CO 5-8615
Coronet	CI 5-9442
Empire	LO 5-7901
Ethel Barrymore	CO 5-9172
48th Street	CO 5-9451
46th Street	CI 5-9455
Fulton	CI 5-9847
Henry Miller	LO 5-8315
Hudson	JU 6-9261
Imperial	CI 5-9374
Lyceum	JU 6-9854
Majestic	CI 5-9353
Mansfield	CI 5-9505
Mark Hellinger	CO 5-9064
Martin Beck	CI 5-9770
Maxine Elliott	LO 5-8583
Metropolitan Opera	PE 6-7200
Morosco	CI 5-9833
Music Box Theatre	CI 5-9850
National	LO 5-8489
New York City Center	CO 5-8933

Plymouth .... CI 5-9474
St. James .... LO 5-8143
Shubert .... CI 6-9500
Winter Garden .... CI 6-9500

CABARETS

* Copacabana .... PL 8-1060

Latin Quarter .... CI 5-9685
    (Theatres and night clubs not listed have no backstage phones.)

* Copacabana's backstage phone is connected to the house switchboard and calls normally are not relayed to the girls. Cagey wolves, however, ask for the Wardrobe Mistress, who is tipped liberally by the chorines to act as the go-between. Quite Parisian, no?

B. TICKET STUBS

Variations from the normal in theatre seating. See page 265.

(NOTE: All houses except where noted eliminate Row I—eye.)

ETHEL BARRYMORE: Row AA precedes Row A.

BELASCO: Row AA precedes Row A.

BIJOU: Row AA precedes Row A.

BOOTH: Row AA precedes Row A.

BROADWAY: Row I is included. Beginning with Row P sequence follows: P, PP, Q, QQ, R, RR, S, SS, T, TT, U.

CARNEGIE HALL: Following Row Z, numbers begin with AA, BB, CC, etc.

CENTURY: Row AA precedes Row A.

CORT: Rows AA and BB precede Row A.

EMPIRE: Row AA precedes Row A.

48TH ST.: Row AA precedes Row A.

FULTON: Row AA precedes Row A.

JOHN GOLDEN: Rows AA, BB and CC precede Row A.

IMPERIAL: Row I is included.

LYCEUM: Row AA precedes Row A.

MAJESTIC: Rows AA and BB precede Row A. I is included.

MANSFIELD: Row AA precedes Row A.

METROPOLITAN OPERA HOUSE: Rows AA and BB precede Row A.

MOROSCO: Row AA precedes Row A.

PLAYHOUSE: Row AA precedes Row A.

PLYMOUTH: Row AA precedes Row A.

ROYALE: Row BB precedes Row A. I is included.

ST. JAMES: Row AA precedes Row A.

WINTER GARDEN: Rows AA and BB precede Row A on sides only.

* * *

Seats numbered 1, 3, 5, 7, etc., and 2, 4, 6, 8, etc., are on the sides of the house, numbers being counted from the center to the wall.

Seats numbered 101, 102, 103, etc., are in the center section of the theatre.

These are the exceptions:

BILTMORE: No center section.

BOOTH: Seats in all three sections are numbered consecutively, 1, 2, 3, etc., being distinguished by "Section 1," for left side of the house, "Section 2," for center, and "Section 3," for right.

CARNEGIE HALL: House has four sections. Seats 1 to 17 are center left, 2 to 18 center right, higher odd numbers, extreme left, and higher even numbers, extreme right.

CORT: Seats in all three sections numbered consecutively, 1, 2, 3, etc., being distinguished by "Right," "Center," and "Left."

JOHN GOLDEN: Two sections only and distinguished by "Right" and "Left."

NEW YORK CITY CENTER: Four sections, seats 1, 3, 5, etc., being extreme left; 2, 4, 6, etc., extreme right; 101, 103, etc., center left; and 102, 104, etc., center right.

C. HEADWAITERS' NAMES

ARMANDO'S: Alfred & Philip
ASTOR HUNTING ROOM: Walter Lindner
BLAIR HOUSE: Christo
BLUE ANGEL: Arturo
COLONY: Gene (prop.)
COPACABANA: Joe Lopez
EL BORACCHO: Attilio
EL MOROCCO: Frank Carino
HAVANA-MADRID: Carlos
LATIN QUARTER: Gigi
LEON & EDDIE'S: Louis
PLAZA PERSIAN ROOM: Fred Barbero
RIVIERA: Bonardi
RUBAN BLEU: Tony Mele (prop.)
ST. REGIS MAISONETTE: August
STORK: Andrew
21: Philip & Pierre
WALDORF: Albert

D. MOVIE COMPANY TALENT SCOUTS

Columbia Pictures, Max Arnow, 729 Seventh Avenue.
Goldwyn, Samuel, Carolyn Stagg, 1270 Avenue of the Americas.
Metro-Goldwyn-Mayer, Al Altman, 1540 Broadway.
Paramount, Boris Kaplan, 1501 Broadway.
RKO-Radio, Arthur Willi, 1270 Avenue of the Americas.
20th Century-Fox, Joe Pincus, 444 West 56th Street.
Universal, Jessica Landau, 1250 Avenue of the Americas.
Warner Bros., Harry Mayer, 321 West 44th Street.

E. GLOSSARY OF HARLEMISMS

A HUMMER: Something better than the ordinary.

ALLIGATOR: A jitterbug.

ARMSTRONGS: High register trumpet notes. (Named after Louis Armstrong.)

BARBECUE: Beautiful gal.

BATTLE: Homely gal.

BEAT or BEAT UP: Exceedingly tired.

BEAT THE CHOPS: To talk.

BIBLE: The truth.

BLACK AND TAN: 1. Varying shades of colored folk. 2. Night club catering to blacks and whites.

BLIP: Classy.

BLOW YOUR TOP: Overcome.

BOOGIE-WOOGIE: Form of harmony with accentuated bass beat.

BREE: A gal.

BUST YOUR CONK: To apply yourself diligently.

CANARY: A gal singer.

CAT: A swing musician.

CHICK: A gal.

CHIME: An hour.

CHIRP: A gal singer.

COLLAR: Obtain or understand.

CUBBY: Room, home.

CUPS: Sleep.

CUT RATE: A cheap guy.

DICTY: Classy, smart.

DIG: Meet or understand.

DIME NOTE: Ten dollar bill.
DOMI: Domicile.
DOSS: Sleep.
DRAPE: Clothes.
DUCHESS: Gal.
DUKE: Hand.
EVIL: Nasty temper.
FEWS AND TWO: Very little money.
FINE DINNER: Pretty gal.
FRAME: The body.
FREEBY: Free.
FROMPY: Homely.
FRONT: Suit of clothes.
FRY: Getting hair straightened.
GAMMIN: Flirting.
GASSER: Terrific.
GATE: A man.
GIMME SOME SKIN: Shake hands.
GLIMS: The eyes.
GOT YOUR GLASSES ON: Being snooty.
GREASE: To eat.
GROOVY: Fine.
HARD: Fine.
HEP CAT: A guy in the know.
HINCTY: Snooty.
HIP: Sophisticated.
HYPE: Trying to sell a bill of goods.
ICKY: A dumb guy.
IGG: To ignore.
IN THE GROOVE: Perfect.
JACK: Common name for all men.
JELLY: Something free.
KICK: Pocket.
KILL ME: Send me.
KILLER-DILLER: A thrill.
KNOCK: Give.

KOPASETIC: The tops.
LATCH ON: Get wise to.
LEAD SHEET: Top coat.
LEFT RAISE: Left side.
LILY WHITES: Bed sheets.
LOCKED UP: Acquiring exclusive possession of something.
MAIN ON THE HITCH: Husband.
MAIN QUEEN: Girl friend.
MASH ME: Give me.
MELLOW: Fine.
MELTED OUT: Broke.
MESS: Something very good.
METER: 25 cents.
MOO JUICE: Milk.
MURDER: Something terrific.
NOD: Sleep.
OFAY: A white person.
OFF THE COBB: Corny.
OUT OF THE WORLD: Perfect.
PASSING: Living as a white person.
PEOLA: Light Negro, almost white.
PIGEON: Young girl.
POUNDERS: Policemen.
QUEEN: Beautiful girl.
READY: Perfect.
RIGHTEOUS: Terrific.
RUG CUTTER: A good dancer.
SAD: Terrible.
SALTY: Angry.
SEND: Arousing emotions.
SHARP: Smart, hep, tricky.
SKY PIECE: Hat.
SLAVE: To work.
SLIDE YOUR JIB: Voluble talk.
SNATCHER: A police detective.
SOLID: Swell.

SQUARE: Opposite of hep.
STACHE: To hide something.
THE MAN: The law.
TICKS: Minutes.
TIMBER: Toothpicks.
TOO MUCH: A term of praise.
TRILLY: To take one's leave.
TRUCK: To go somewhere.
TWISTER: Key.
V-8: An independent gal.
WHIPPED UP: Tired.
WREN: A female.

F. GUSTATORY GUIDE

DINE WITHOUT ORCHESTRAL DIN:
    Café Impériale, 322 E. 44th.
    Dinty Moore's, 216 W. 46th (Famous for steaks, corned beef & cabbage).
    Toots Shor's, 51 W. 51st.
    Lindy's, B'way & 50th.
    Sardi's, 234 W. 44th.
    Twenty One, 21 W. 52nd (If you can get in).
    Stork Club Cub Room, 3 E. 53rd (Ditto).
    Colony, Madison & 61st (Ditto).
    Cavanagh's, 258 W. 23rd.
    Reuben's, 6 E. 58th (Where the late crowd goes).
    Barberry Room, 19 E. 52nd.
    Al Schacht's, 104 E. 52nd (Owned by the baseball clown).

Gallagher's, 228 W. 52nd.

Artists & Writers, 213 W. 40th (Grub Street).

Blair House, 30 W. 56th.

Q Club, 302 E. 58th.

Lee Chumley's, 86 Bedford (Village bohemian newspaper hangout).

Billy the Oysterman, 10 W. 47th; 7 E. 20th.

Charles, 452 Sixth Ave. (Expensive).

INSTRUMENTAL MUSIC AT DINNER, NO DANCING:

Little Club, 70 E. 55th.

Luchow's, 110 E. 14th.

El Boraccho, 51 E. 55th.

El Morocco Champagne Room, 154 E. 54th.

Penthouse, 30 W. 59th.

Armando's, 54 E. 55th.

DINING AROUND THE WORLD:

ARMENIAN:

Golden Horn, 31 W. 51st.

AUSTRIAN:

Mayerling, 133 E. 54th.

Hapsburg House, 313 E. 55th.

Gay Vienna, 1611 Second Ave.

Grinzing, 323 E. 79th.

BALKAN:

The Balkan, 294 Eighth Ave.

BELGIAN:

Brussels, 26 E. 63rd (Beaucoup expensive).

CHINESE:

Lum Fong, 150 W. 52nd.

House of Chan, 800 Seventh Ave. (52nd).

Yank Sing, 133 W. 51st (Show folk hangout).

Canton Village, 163 W. 49th.

Ding Ho, 103 W. 49th.

Hoy Yuen, 117 W. 48th.

Tung Sai, Mulberry St. (Shavey Lee, Mayor of Chinatown, prop.).

China Lane, Mott St.

Chinese Rathskeller, Mott St.

Ho Ho, Seventh Ave. & 51st.

CUBAN:

Cuban Casino, 45th & Eighth Ave. (Floor show).

CZECHOSLOVAK:

Praha, 1358 First Ave.

DUTCH:

Holland House Taverne, 10 Rockefeller Pl.

EGYPTIAN:

Port Said, 257 W. 29th.

ENGLISH:

Keen's, 72 W. 36th.

Drury Lane, 47 E. 49th.

FRENCH:

Lafayette, University Pl. & 9th.

Roberto's, 22 E. 46th.

Voisin, 375 Park Ave.

Marguery, 270 Park Ave.

Chambord, Third Ave. & 50th.

Larue, 45 E. 58th (Dancing).

Charles, 452 Sixth Ave.

Coq Rouge, 65 E. 56th (Dancing).

Janet of France, 237 W. 52nd (Entertainment).

Café Arnold, Columbus Circle.

Café Louis XIV, 15 W. 49th.

Caviar, 18 E. 49th.

Chateaubriand, 148 E. 56th.

Divan Parisien, 17 E. 45th.

La Cava, 128 W. 52nd.

La Salle du Bois, 36 E. 60th.

Theodore's, 4 E. 56th.

Bal Tabarin, 225 W. 46th (Floor show).

GREEK:
Acropolis, 312 W. 58th.

GYPSY:
Gypsy Tea Kettle, 50th & Seventh Ave. (Tea leaves read).
Romany Marie, 49 Grove (Village).
Golden Earring, 54th & Madison Ave.

HAWAIIAN:
Hawaiian Room, Lexington Hotel (48th) (With hula girls).

HINDU:
East India Curry Shop, 52 E. 55th.
India Rajah, 235 W. 48th.
Famous India Curry Rice, 34 W. 114th.
India Prince, W. 47th.

HUNGARIAN:
Tokay, 1591 Second Ave.
Zimmerman's Hungaria, 163 W. 46th (Floor show).

IRISH:
Hogan's, 235 W. 52nd.

ITALIAN:
Villanova, 106 W. 46th.
Cerutti's, 643 Madison Ave.
Buscaglia, 33 W. 46th.
Leone's, 239 W. 48th.
Little Venice, 126 W. 13th.
Eddie's Aurora, 144 W. 4th (Ingrid Bergman ate here).
Enrico & Paglieri, 64 W. 11th.

JAPANESE:
Miyako, 20 W. 56th.
Suyehiro, 35 E. 29th.

MEXICAN:
Charro El Mexican, 4 Charles (Village).
El Nilo, 108 W. 44th.

ROMANIAN:
Old Romania, Allen St. (Lower East Side. Floor show).

Russian:
  Casino Russe, 157 W. 56th (Entertainment).
  Russian Tea Room, 150 W. 57th (Hangout for musical
    long hairs).
  Russian Kretchma, 244 E. 14th (Floor show).
  Russian Bear, 645 Lexington (Entertainment).
Scandinavian:
  Iceland, Broadway & 53rd (Floor show).
  Wivel, 254 W. 54th (Floor show).
  Stockholm, 27 W. 51st.
  Kungsholm, 142 E. 55th.
  Castleholm, 244 W. 57th.
Singhalese:
  Ceylon India Inn, 148 W. 49th.
South Seas:
  Singapore, Broadway & 51st (Also Chinese).
Spanish:
  Havana Madrid, Broadway & 51st (Floor show).
  Las Americas, 687 Lexington.
  El Caserio, 145 E. 55th.
  El Chico, Sheridan Sq. (Floor show).
Swiss:
  Swiss Pavilion, 38 E. 50th.
  La Petite Suisse, 6 W. 52nd.
Syrian:
  Mecca, 6 E. 30th.
Yiddish:
  Moskowitz & Lupowitz, 40 Second Ave.
  Lou Siegel, 209 W. 38th.
  Paramount, 138 W. 43rd.
  Gluckstern, 209 W. 48th.

SUMMER ONLY:
  Al fresco:
    St. Moritz Hotel, Central Park So.
    Fifth Avenue Hotel, Fifth & 9th.

Chatham Walk, Vanderbilt & 48th.
Rockefeller Center Plaza.
Central Park Zoo Terrace.
Ambassador Garden.

ROOF GARDENS:
Waldorf Starlight Roof.
Astor.
Pennsylvania.
Biltmore.

CITY ROAD HOUSES:
Bill Miller's Riviera (across George Washington Bridge).
Tavern-on-the-Green, Central Park.

ENVIRONS:
Ray Dillman's Casino-in-the-Park, Jersey City (Beautiful and swank).
Casa Seville, Franklin Sq., L. I. (Fabulous).